The Great Awakening

Primary Sources in
American History

CONSULTING EDITOR
Grady McWhiney, University of British Columbia

The Great Awakening

The Beginnings of Evangelical
Pietism in America

EDITED BY **J. M. BUMSTED**
Simon Fraser University

BLAISDELL PUBLISHING COMPANY
A Division of Ginn and Company
WALTHAM, MASSACHUSETTS / TORONTO / LONDON

Foreword

Thorough understanding of the events and trends that make up our history cannot be acquired merely by reading textbook interpretations. It is essential also to study the basis of such interpretations. *The Primary Sources in American History Series* provides the student with materials in the form of letters, diaries, memoirs, pamphlets, and newspaper accounts written during or shortly after major historical events — documents up to now buried in the library and often unavailable.

Edited and introduced by a leading scholar, each volume either concentrates on discussion of a given topic in contemporary letters, newspaper articles, and essays or presents new editions of classic eyewitness accounts of significant events. Though generations removed from an actual occurrence, the student has the opportunity to understand it in depth and to apply his analytical and critical powers to it. He then also can compare his own interpretations with those provided by general histories, biographies, and monographs.

GRADY MCWHINEY

Preface

In the following pages the reader will find a number of representative documents illustrative of the Great Awakening in colonial America. No one is more conscious than I of the limitations of such a selection. It is impossible even in several hundred pages to do justice to the manifold themes and issues inherent in this fascinating and important phenomenon, which one historian has called "America's first national experience." The documents I have selected represent my own assessment of importance and interest, and the reader should keep this fact firmly in mind. In general, I have attempted to choose documents which illustrate what I consider to be the major themes of the Awakening. Because the majority of readers are probably most familiar with the revival in literary and intellectual terms — scholarly study of it has been biased in this way — I have consciously emphasized an institutional and social context and employed readings taken to a large extent from sources other than the sermons of those contemporaries so commonly associated with the event. I have provided only minimal editorial comment, attempting to indicate in brief introductions why I included a given document and where it fits into the larger picture. The reader will undoubtedly discover that a good deal of the material contained in the following selections requires further illumination. I trust he will not hesitate to turn to an ever-growing body of secondary literature for answers to perplexing questions; few historians that I know work solely from the "sources."

J. M. BUMSTED

Contents

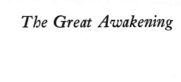

The Great Awakening

CHAPTER 1 The Background of
the Great Awakening

The "great and general revival of religion" usually called the
Great Awakening did not really begin in America until after
the arrival of George Whitefield in the colonies in 1739. The
revival cannot be properly understood without some notion of
the forces, both religious and secular, which underlay the seem-
ingly sudden explosion of spiritual concern in America beginning in 1740.

The general movement of "experimental" (that is, experienced) religion and evangelical piety of which the Awakening
was a part did not originate in the New World, but was rather
a product of Europe in the seventeenth century. Responses
among Protestants in Germany particularly critical were to the
dislocations of the Thirty Years War and to an increasingly for-
malized religious establishment. A large number of German
pietistic sects sprung up and an enormous devotional literature
was generated, much of which (such as the works of August
Francke) circulated rather widely in Europe and even reached
America. In England, devotional works of German pietists like
Francke and Philipp Spener struck a particularly respondent
chord within certain circles of the Anglican Church associated
with the nonjurying Anglican clergyman William Law, whose
followers included John and Charles Wesley as well as George
Whitefield. Both the German pietists — many of whom emigrated to America in the eighteenth century in search of peace

1

and toleration — and the English evangelical stream which later became Methodism brought to the colonies a developed movement of pietistic commitment and spiritual concern.

In America, the early eighteenth century saw an increasing perception by clergymen that religion was "dead" and sterile, that Americans did not bother sufficiently with important questions such as the salvation of their souls. This sense of religious "declension" had begun in Puritan New England in the previous century and led to enormous quantities of "jeremiads," sermons predicting imminent doom if the populace did not reform. By 1740, most colonial clergymen were preaching jeremiads to an audience that still had a firm intellectual if not emotional commitment to religion. Both ministers and people wanted revival, and indeed, a number of clergymen were successful before 1740 in their own local communities in tapping the popular craving for meaningful spiritual experiences. For the most part, these local revivals were indigeniously American, based upon peculiarly American religious practice and needs and owing virtually nothing to the Old World currents already stirring.

The preaching tour of George Whitefield in the colonies from 1739 to 1741 merged Old World pietism with an American concern and search for just such a spiritual movement at an especially critical and tense time. Life seemed to be going badly or boding ill for large numbers of colonials at the end of the 1730's. Easily available land in the seacoast regions seemed to be vanishing rapidly, and the American economy was limited by the absense of an adequate circulating medium of exchange which led to popular demands for an easy money policy of paper currency; in New England, the crisis over currency reached its peak almost synonymously with Whitefield's arrival in the region. In addition to economic difficulties, Americans worried about extension of a war which had already begun between England and Spain; if France were drawn into the conflict, there would be increased evidence of Indian raids, recruiting of soldiers and impressment of seamen, and even threats of armed invasion for some areas. Concerned over the potential death and destruction of war, the colonists realized to their dismay that the number of particularly fatal epidemics of communicable diseases seemed higher than ever before. In a variety of ways, Americans were distressed and concerned about the future in 1740, and given the religious upbringing of most, it is hardly surprising that they would find some comfort and assurance in a spiritual message which told them not to worry about the present and offered them eternal salvation. It was just such a message which George Whitefield offered.

The rebirth of a "spirit of vital piety" in Protestantism began in seventeenth-century Germany with the growth of a variety of small sects such as the Moravians. Like most rigorous pietists, these groups tended to clash with religious establishments and civil authorities, and many of them sought greater spiritual and economic freedom by emigrating to British North America, especially the colonies of Pennsylvania, Georgia, and the Carolinas. These sects introduced various British religious leaders in both the New and Old World to new spiritual values, and they provided a tradition of religious awakening upon which later popular evangelists could build. The following selection recounts early Moravian beginnings in America.

A History of the Beginnings of Moravian Work in America, W. N. Schwarze and S. H. Gapp, compilers and translators.
Bethlehem, Pennsylvania, 1955, pp. 5, 9, 10–14

["*Brief Treatise Concerning the Initial Spread of the Moravian and Bohemian Brethren in the North-American Colonies and Missions from the year 1732 to 1741*"]

1.

The Brethren emigrating from Moravia and Bohemia since 1722, who had turned toward Upper Lusatia, had found asylum on the estates of Count Nicolaus Ludwig von Zinzendorf and had built Herrnhut, had sung already in November, 1727:

> Herrnhut shall not longer stand
>   Than the Words of His hand
> *Unhindered* therein go:
>   And love be the bond
> Until we prepared
> And ready to serve
> As a good *salt of the earth*
> Are usefully *spread abroad,*

Hence, at that time already, after they had experienced on the 13th of August of the same year a special baptism of the Spirit at a Communion service, their thought was directed to their dispersion especially into regions of the world where the name of Christ was not yet known, or but little known. Whereto among other things this circumstance also gave occasion that the Court of Electoral Saxony, in the year 1732, forbade all the landed estates of Upper Lusatia to receive alien subjects of Bohemia, Moravia and Silesia, since the Moravian exiles still expected quite a number of their Brethren to follow them, for whom asylum must be considered. Hence the Moravian Brethren, since the Commission of 1732, reflected upon colonies and missions, where they might secure for themselves and the Brethren still following them from Bohemia and Moravia sojourn with maintenance of their church rights and liberties, to bear fruit among Christians and heathen, wherever the divine ordaining might place and plant them.

* * *

8.

There went also to this Province Mr. Edward James Oglethorpe, at that time under appointment as Governor of Georgia, together with quite a number of English families as also three clergymen of the English High Church, namely, John Wesley, and his brother, Charles Wesley, priests, also Benjamin Ingham, ord[ained] Deacon, and Charles Delamotte, a school-teacher.

John Wesley at once made himself acquainted with the Brethren, learned from them some German, as some of them English from him. Since the clergyman [Ordinarius] of Savanna, Mr. Quincey, continued still to occupy the rectory here for some time, John Wesley, together with Charles Delamotte moved to the Brethren in their house on Wednesday the 25 February/8 March until after his departure, on the 15 March/ 26 March, he could move into the rectory. Since he could understand German quite well, he attended all the worship services of the Brethren. He began also to translate some of the hymns of the Herrnhut hymnal into English, and some of these have come into the English hymnals of the Brethren. . . .

13.

Now Br. David Nitschmann and A. G. Spangenberg had come to Pennsylvania, in the spring of 1736. The former indeed intended to gather an accurate report concerning conditions in this land and to see what should be done for the extension of Christ's Kingdom, and also especially to go on a visitation to St. Thomas to impart holy ordination to Br. Friederich Martin and to discharge other necessary business awaiting the visitor. However he was prevented from carrying out this journey through reports received by letter from Europe and he assigned the visitation to Brother A. G. Spangenberg, who undertook the same and discharged it. During his [Nitschmann's] stay in Pennsylvania, in the months of April, May and June, he became acquainted with many godly persons and in New York too with various sincere spirits. By him Br. Spangenberg wrote from New York, in June, to Br. Ludwig [Zinzendorf] in Europe and urged upon him a visit to Pennsylavnia. See, Br. Ludwig's "Communication to His Dear Germans," p. 15, 4th Supplement.

14.

Spangenberg had been sent to Pennsylvania by the church [Gemeine] really in the interests of the Schwenkfelder, who had asked the church [Gemeine] for a couple of Brethren to minister to their own physical and spiritual well-being and in addition to see that a way might be prepared for the Lord should He grant this land to experience a gracious visitation. The Moravian Brother Böhnisch had journeyed to Pennsylvania with the Schwenkfelder in 1734 with the above mentioned intention. Spangenberg as well as Böhnisch had stayed at Christoph Wiegners', a Schwenkfelder family in Schippach, to whom also a Görlitzer friend of the Brethren, by the name of Christoph Paus, who had come into the country with the Schwenkfelder, had likewise betaken himself. This company at that time constituted a small church in their home; and because in their sincere aim they made themselves acquainted with many upright souls of various persuasions, they drew the attention of many persons to themselves and received visits from those near and far. Upon Br. Spangenberg's summons, Georg Neisser (who was to have accompanied him and Br. Nitschmann to Pennsylvania in the previous year, but had been hindered, and who was also to have accompanied Br. Spangenberg to St. Thomas, but the letters were received too late) came to Pennsylvania in the spring of 1737 and likewise to the aforesaid Wiegner family.

15.

As a concession to the Schwenkfelder, this whole company attended their meeting and accommodated themselves to their habit of dress as well as to other externals in so far as possible. But as it became evident that such a concession together with friendly approaches and other efforts that had been made, would not bear fruit in winning them, we gradually withdrew from them. . . . Since Br. George Böhnisch had left his wife in Herrnhut, when he journeyed hither, he returned to Europe anno 1737.

16.

Since, now, in the two years 1736, 1737 to 1738, Br. Spangenberg and the other Brethren dwelling together at Christoph Wiegner's made the blessed acquaintanceship of upright souls in

the neighborhood of Schippach and other places, as Philadelphia, Germantown, Matetsche, Falkner's Swamp, Oley, also in
Canastoga, they received many a visit from people of varied
persuasions: Baptists, Quakers, the Sabbatarians [Adventists] of
Ephrata, and Separatists. Spangenberg and Christoph Wiegner
at one time made an important visit [*Haupt Besuch*] in Falkner's Swamp, Oley, and in Canastoga, among the people of
Ephrata, and the so-called New Mooners in Canastoga Swamp,
at the house of Johannes Zimmermann, etc., and found many
upright souls, who however were divided and separated because of vagaries and minor matters.

The people of Ephrata, whom the Brethren Spangenberg and
his Associated Brethren visited several times, once expressed
themselves through three of their number to the effect that they
believed indeed that the Brethren in Europe were the visible
Eastern Church of God, but that here in America they (the
Ephrataner] were the Western Church of God. Hence they
desired to learn whether Spangenberg with his Brethren would
establish their own household of faith and closed communion.
They would however rather advise them, yes summon them,
to unite themselves with them and to enter their fellowship,
because they had the call to gather the children of God.

17.

Since there has been mention of the *Tunkers* and the people
of Ephrata as churchly societies in Pennsylvania, especially as
the Brethren in succeeding years had some intercourse with
these people, it may be useful to insert some report of them.
[Compare *Chronicon Ephratense* on this.]

The *Tunker*-sects [i.e. Immersionists] had emerged and had
their beginning in the years 1715 and following in Germany, in
the Palatinate, Switzerland, etc. They distinguished themselves
from the Mennonites in their manner of baptism, in that they
upheld complete immersion and submersion of adult candidates
for baptism; also foot-washing according to John XIII; the restoration of all things and other teachings and doctrines taken over

from the Pietists. They were on that account persecuted in their communities and some went to Ordenburg and Schwarzenau, where they were unable to get along with the Separatists and the *Inspired;* some removed to Crevelt and some to Holland. When then the report concerning Pennsylvania and the freedom of conscience here to be enjoyed had been spread abroad to Germany, and various of the Pietists and Separatists, who were oppressed because of religion, had removed hither, the greater part of them also removed here to Pennsylvania and West Jersey. Here they sought at once to make proselytes and found ready approach to well-intentioned spirits. The remaining Protestant religious people (especially in view of their extremely wretched condition) were severely attacked by them and held in scorn.

From these *Tunkers* a group separated themselves under the leadership of Conrad Beissel, who had formerly belonged to the Inspired. They built a community on the Cocalico in Canastoga which they named Ephrata. They adopted the Gichtelian and Ueberfeldian principles; began to observe Saturday as Sabbath instead of Sunday; distinguished themselves because they elected the monastic and cloister life, also by means of a cloister habit; led a very strict life with castigation, night-watches and abstinence from certain foods; began a common life (*communionem bonorum*) and through their varied pecularities attracted much attention among varied people. With it all they were very active and devoted in untiring effort to make proselytes to their way of thinking and manner of life and often went out for enlistment not only in this but also in neighboring Provinces. Wherever they have been able to find awakened souls somewhat persuaded of the truth, they looked them up, made them to be doubtful concerning their course hitherto, sought to make all other religions [in the sense of religious denominations] open to suspicion and their modes of worship distasteful and insipid; praised, on the other hand, their own way and constitution and summoned them urgently and with most vigorous importunity to enter their own communion, because they were the American or Western Church of God and had the vocation of God to gather the scattered children of God.

Now they were, indeed, rejected in their testimony by some, and especially by a certain enlightened man, who had for many years walked in the ways of God and stood in love and good understanding with all the children and servants of God known to him and with the precedent noted in Joshua 17: 14–18, according to the mystic application. For he gave them to understand, that if they would increase their fellowship they should seek their salvation among the crude multitude of the children of the world. But with those lacking the firm foundation and not fully established, though awakened souls, they attained their purpose. For as religion on the pietistic basis, with most people, had developed into all manner of penitence practices and self-originated efforts, they found sufficiency of these in the Ephrata Society, and a considerable number of souls were carried away with incredible swiftness by this seeming religiousness so that there was the prospect that they would in the course of time constitute the chief sect of this land. Even one of our Brethren, Gottfried Haberecht, about the year 1739, who had come from Georgia to Pennsylvania in 1738, went over to their fellowship. [Note. Later he returned to the Moravians.] Especially among Baptists they enticed away many of their people.

But the few Brethren who knew in whom they believed, already belonged to a visible orthodox church and were people of His possession, were assured also of the purpose of their Church's Head to plant them in Pennsylvania, remained standing immovably on the foundation of their faith, to the shaking of which every thinkable effort was given. . . .

One of the British groups most influenced by continental pietism was the small circle at Oxford University which included the Wesleys (John and Charles) and George Whitefield. Nominally Anglican, this group responded favorably not only to the Germans but to a more native devotionalism spearheaded by William Law. The dynamics of the process of awakening are here detailed by George Whitefield.

GEORGE WHITEFIELD
George Whitefield's Journals.
London, The Banner of Truth Trust, 1960, pp. 42–49

[*"A Short Account of God's Dealings With the Reverend Mr.
George Whitefield . . . Written by Himself"*]

1732–1734

But all this while I continued in secret sin; and, at length, got
acquainted with such a set of debauched, abandoned, atheistical
youths, that if God, by His free, unmerited, and especial grace,
had not delivered me out of their hands, I should have long since
sat in the scorner's chair, and made a mock at sin. By keeping
company with them, my thoughts of religion grew more and
more like theirs. I went to public service only to make sport
and walk about. I took pleasure in their lewd conversation. I
began to reason as they did, and to ask why God had given me
passions, and not permitted me to gratify them? Not considering that God did not originally give us these *corrupt* passions,
and that He had promised help to withstand them, if we would
ask it of Him. In short, I soon made a great proficiency in the
school of the Devil. I affected to look rakish, and was in a fair
way of being as infamous as the worst of them.

But, oh stupendous love! God even here stopped me, when
running on in a full career to hell. For, just as I was upon the
brink of ruin, He gave me such a distaste of their principles and
practices, that I discovered them to my master, who soon put
a stop to their proceedings.

Being thus delivered out of the snare of the Devil, I began to
be more and more serious, and felt God at different times working powerfully and convincingly upon my soul. One day in
particular, as I was coming downstairs, and overheard my
friends speaking well of me, God so deeply convicted me of
hypocrisy, that though I had formed frequent but ineffectual
resolutions before, yet I had then power given me over my

secret and darling sin. Notwithstanding, some time after being overtaken in liquor, as I have been twice or thrice in my lifetime, Satan gained his usual advantage over me again, — an experimental proof to my poor soul, how that wicked one makes use of men as machines, working them up to just what he pleases, when by intemperance they have chased away the Spirit of God from them.

Being now near the seventeenth year of my age, I was resolved to prepare myself for the holy Sacrament, which I received on Christmas Day. I began now to be more and more watchful over my thoughts, words, and actions. I kept the following Lent, fasting Wednesday and Friday thirty-six hours together. My evenings, when I had done waiting upon my mother, were generally spent in acts of devotion, reading *Drelincourt on Death,* and other practical books, and I constantly went to public worship twice a day. Being now upperboy, by God's help I made some reformation amongst my schoolfellows. I was very diligent in reading and learning the classics, and in studying my Greek Testament, but was not yet convinced of the absolute unlawfulness of playing at cards, and of reading and seeing plays, though I began to have some scruples about it.

Near this time I dreamed that I was to see God on Mount Sinai, but was afraid to meet Him. This made a great impression upon me; and a gentlewoman to whom I told it, said, "George, this is a call from God."

Still I grew more serious after this dream; but yet hypocrisy crept into every action. As once I affected to look more rakish, I now strove to appear more grave than I really was. However, an uncommon concern and alteration was visible in my behaviour, and I often used to find fault with the lightness of others.

One night, as I was going on an errand for my mother, an unaccountable, but very strong impression was made upon my heart that I should preach quickly. When I came home, I innocently told my mother what had befallen me; but she, like Joseph's parents, when he told them his dream, turned short upon me, crying out: "What does the boy mean? Prithee hold thy tongue," or something to that purpose. God has since shown her from Whom that impression came.

For a twelve month, I went on in a round of duties, receiving the Sacrament monthly, fasting frequently, attending constantly on public worship, and praying often more than twice a day in private. One of my brothers used to tell me, he feared this would not hold long, and that I should forget all when I came to Oxford. This caution did me much service, for it set me upon praying for perseverance; and, under God, the preparation I made in the country was a preservative against the manifold temptations which beset me at my first coming to that seat of learning.

Being now near eighteen years old, it was judged proper for me to go to the University. God had sweetly prepared my way. My friends before applied to recommended me to the Master of Pembroke College. Another friend took up £10 upon bond, which I have since repaid, to defray the first expense of entering; and the Master, contrary to all expectations, admitted me servitor immediately.

Soon after my admission I went and resided, and found my having been used to a public-house was now of service to me. For many of the servitors being sick at my first coming up, by my diligent and ready attendance, I ingratiated myself into the gentlemen's favour so far, that many, who had it in their power, chose me to be their servitor.

This much lessened my expense; and indeed, God was so gracious, that with the profits of my place, and some little presents made me by my kind tutor, for almost the first three years I did not put all my relations together to above £24 expense. And it has often grieved my soul to see so many young students spending their substance in extravagant living, and thereby entirely unfitting themselves for the prosecution of their studies.

I had not been long at the University, before I found the benefit of the foundation I had laid in the country for a holy life. I was quickly solicited to join in their excess of riot with several who lay in the same room. God, in answer to prayers before put up, gave me grace to withstand them; and once in particular, it being cold, my limbs were so benumbed by sitting alone in my study, because I would not go out amongst them, that I could scarce sleep all night. But I soon found the benefit of not yielding: for when they perceived they could not prevail, they let me alone as a singular odd fellow.

All this while I was not fully satisfied of the sin of playing at cards and reading plays, till God upon a fast-day was pleased to convince me. For, taking a play, to read a passage out of it to a friend, God struck my heart with such power, that I was obliged to lay it down again; and, blessed be His Name, I have not read any such book since.

Before I went to the University, I met with Mr. Law's *Serious Call to a Devout Life*, but had not then money to purchase it. Soon after my coming up to the University, seeing a small edition of it in a friend's hand, I soon procured it. God worked powerfully upon my soul, as He has since upon many others, by that and his other excellent treatise upon *Christian Perfection*.

I now began to pray and sing psalms thrice every day, besides morning and evening, and to fast every Friday, and to receive the Sacrament at a parish church near our college, and at the castle, where the despised Methodists used to receive once a month.

The young men so called were then much talked of at Oxford. I had heard of, and loved them before I came to the University; and so strenuously defended them when I heard them reviled by the students, that they began to think that I also in time should be one of them.

For above a twelvemonth my soul longed to be acquainted with some of them, and I was strongly pressed to follow their good example, when I saw them go through a ridiculing crowd to receive the Holy Eucharist at St. Mary's. At length, God was pleased to open a door. It happened that a poor woman in one of the workhouses had attempted to cut her throat, but was happily prevented. Upon hearing of this, and knowing that both the Mr. Wesleys were ready to every good work, I sent a

poor apple-woman of our college to inform Mr. Charles Wesley
of it, charging her not to discover who sent her. She went; but,
contrary to my orders, told my name. He having heard of my
coming to the castle and a parish-church sacrament, and having
met me frequently walking by myself, followed the woman
when she was gone away, and sent an invitation to me by her,
to come to breakfast with him the next morning.

I thankfully embraced the opportunity; and, blessed be God!
it was one of the most profitable visits I ever made in my life.
My soul, at that time, was athirst for some spiritual friends to
lift up my hands when they hung down, and to strengthen my
feeble knees. He soon discovered it, and, like a wise winner of
souls, made all his discourses tend that way. And when he had
put into my hands Professor Francke's treatise *Against the Fear
of Man*, and a book, entitled, *The Country Parson's Advice to
His Parishioners* (the last of which was wonderfully blessed to
my soul) I took my leave.

In a short time he let me have another book, entitled, *The
Life of God in the Soul of Man;* and, though I had fasted,
watched and prayed, and received the Sacrament so long, yet
I never knew what true religion was, till God sent me that excellent treatise by the hands of my never-to-be-forgotten friend.

At my first reading it, I wondered what the author meant by
saying, "That some falsely placed religion in going to church,
doing hurt to no one, being constant in the duties of the closet,
and now and then reaching out their hands to give alms to their
poor neighbours," "Alas!" thought I, "if this be not true religion, what is?" God soon showed me; for in reading a few
lines further, that "true religion was union of the soul with
God, and Christ formed within us," a ray of Divine light was
instantaneously darted in upon my soul, and from that moment,
but not till then, did I know that I must be a new creature.

Upon this, like the woman of Samaria, when Christ revealed
Himself to her at the well I had no rest in my soul till I wrote
letters to my relations, telling them there was such a thing as
the new birth. I imagined they would have gladly received it.

But, alas! my words seemed to them as idle tales. They thought that I was going beside myself, and by their letters, confirmed me in the resolutions I had taken not to go down into the country, but continue where I was, lest, by any means the good work which God had begun in my soul might be made of none effect.

From time to time Mr. Wesley permitted me to come unto him, and instructed me as I was able to bear it. By degrees he introduced me to the rest of his Christian brethren. They built me up daily in the knowledge and fear of God, and taught me to endure hardness like a good soldier of Jesus Christ.

I now began, like them, to live by rule, and to pick up the very fragments of my time, that not a moment of it might be lost. Whether I ate or drank, or whatsoever I did, I endeavoured to do all to the glory of God. Like them, having no weekly sacrament, although the Rubric required it, at our own college, I received every Sunday at Christ Church. I joined with them in keeping the stations by fasting Wednesdays and Fridays and left no means unused, which I thought would lead me nearer to Jesus Christ.

Regular retirement, morning and evening, at first I found some difficulty in submitting to; but it soon grew profitable and delightful. As I grew ripe for such exercises, I was from time to time engaged to visit the sick and the prisoners, and to read to poor people, till I made it a custom, as much of us did, to spend an hour every day in doing acts of charity.

The course of my studies I soon entirely changed. Whereas, before, I was busied in studying the dry sciences, and books that went no farther than the surface, I now resolved to read only such as entered into the heart of religion, and which led me directly into an experimental knowledge of Jesus Christ, and Him crucified. The lively oracles of God were my soul's delight. The book of the Divine laws was seldom out of my hands: I meditated therein day and night; and ever since that, God has made my way signally prosperous, and given me abundant success.

God enabled me to do much good to many, as well as to receive much from the despised Methodists, and made me instrumental in converting one who is lately come into the Church, and, I trust, will prove a burning and a shining light.

Several short fits of illness was God pleased to visit and to try me with after my first acquaintance with Mr. Wesley. My new convert was a help-meet for me in those and in all other circumstances; and, in company with him, and several other Christian friends, did I spend many sweet and delightful hours. Never did persons, I believe, strive more earnestly to enter in at the strait gate. They kept their bodies under even to an extreme. They were dead to the world, and willing to be accounted as the dung and offscouring of all things, so that they might win Christ. Their hearts glowed with the love of God, and they never prospered so much in the inward man, as when they had all manner of evil spoken against them falsely without.

Many came amongst them for a while, who, in time of temptation, fell away. The displeasure of a tutor or Head of a College, the changing of a gown from a lower to a higher degree — above all, a thirst for the praise of men, more than that which cometh from God, and a servile fear of contempt — caused numbers that had set their hand to the plough, shamefully to look back. The world, and not themselves, gave them the title of Methodists, I suppose, from their custom of regulating their time, and planning the business of the day every-morning. Mr. John and Charles Wesley, were two of the first that thus openly dared to confess Christ; and they, under God, were the spiritual fathers of most of them. They had the pleasure of seeing the work of the Lord prosper in their hands before they went to Georgia. Since their return, the small grain of mustard-seed has sprung up apace. It has taken deep root. It is growing into a great tree. Ere long, I trust, it will fill the land, and numbers of souls will come from the East and from the West, from the North and from the South, and lodge under the branches of it.

The perception of spiritual decline was uncommonly strong all over British North America in the early eighteenth century. From Puritan New England to Quaker Pennsylvania to Anglican South Carolina, clergymen bewailed lax beliefs and loose behavior. The following statement from the Pennsylvania Presbyterian leader, Samuel Blair, illustrates prevailing clerical sentiment.

JOSEPH TRACY

A History of the Revival of Religion in the Time of Edwards and Whitefield.

Boston, 1842, pp. 24–26

August 6th, 1744.

That it may the more clearly appear that the Lord has indeed carried on a work of true real religion among us of late years, I conceive it will be useful to give a brief general view of the state of religion in these parts before this remarkable season. I doubt not, then, but there were some sincerely religious people up and down; and there were, I believe, a considerable number in the several congregations pretty exact, according to their education, in the observance of the external forms of religion, not only as to attendance upon public ordinances on the Sabbaths, but also, as to the practice of family worship, and perhaps, secret prayer too. But with these things the most part seemed to appearance to rest contented; and to satisfy their consciences just with a dead formality in religion. If they performed these duties pretty punctually in their seasons, and as they thought with a good meaning out of conscience, and not just to obtain a name for religion among men; then they were ready to conclude that they were truly and sincerely religious. A very lamentable ignorance of the main essentials of true practical religion and the doctrines nextly relating thereunto, very generally prevailed. The nature and necessity of the new birth was but little known or thought of. The necessity of a conviction of sin and misery, by the Holy Spirit opening and applying the Law to the conscience, in order to a saving closure with Christ, was hardly known at all to the most. It was thought that if there was any need of a heart-distressing sight of the soul's danger, and fear of divine wrath, it was only needful for the grosser sort of sinners; and for any others to be deeply exercised this way, (as there might sometimes be before some rare instances observable,) this was generally looked up to be a great evil and temptation that had befallen those persons. The common names for such soul-concern were melancholy, trouble of mind, or despair. These terms were in common, so far as I have been acquainted, indifferently used as synonymous; and trouble of mind was looked upon as a great evil, which all persons that made any sober profession and practice of religion ought carefully to avoid. There was scarcely any suspicion at all, in general, of any danger of depending upon self-righteousness, and not upon the righteousness of Christ alone for salvation. Papists and Quakers would be readily acknowledged guilty of this crime; but hardly any professed Presbyterian. The necessity of being first in Christ by a vital union, and in a justified state, before our religious services can be well pleasing and acceptable to God, was very little understood or thought of. But the common notion seemed to be, that if people were aiming to be in the way of duty as well as they could, as they imagined, there was no reason to be much afraid.

According to these principles, and this ignorance of some of the most soul-concerning truths of the Gospel, people were very generally, through the land, careless at heart, and stupidly indifferent about the great concerns of eternity. There was very little appearance of any hearty engagedness in religion; and indeed the wise, for the most part, were in a great degree asleep with the foolish. It was sad to see with what a careless behaviour the public ordinances were attended, and how people were given to unsuitable wordly discourse on the Lord's holy day. In public companies, especially at weddings, a vain and frothy lightness was apparent in the deportment of many professors; and in some places very extravagant follies, as horse-running, fiddling and dancing, pretty much obtained on those occasions.

Thus religion lay as it were dying, and ready to expire its last breath of life in this part of the visible church. . . .

An assessment of the spiritual state of the American colonies in 1740 is provided in the following extract from the journals of George Whitefield.

GEORGE WHITEFIELD
George Whitefield's Journals.
London, The Banner of Truth Trust, 1960, pp. 386–389

Wednesday, Jan. 9, [*1740*]

I think it may not be amiss to put down some remarks which I have lately passed through. And here I cannot but give Pennsylvania the preference. To me it seems to be the garden of America. Their oxen are strong to labour, and there seems to be no complaining in their streets. What is best of all, I believe they have the Lord for their God. This, I infer, from their having so many faithful ministers sent forth amongst them; and, except Northampton in New England, the work of conversion has not been carried on with so much power in any part of America, that I can hear of, as under the ministry of Messrs. Tennents, Cross, and the other labourers before mentioned. The Constitution is far from being arbitrary; the soil is good, the land exceedingly fruitful, and there is a greater equality between the poor and rich than perhaps can be found in any other place of the known world. For my part, I like it so well, that, God willing, I purpose taking up some land to erect a school for negroes, and settle some of my English friends, whose hearts God shall stir up, or whom the fury of their enemies shall oblige to depart from their native land.

Philadelphia is one of the most regular planned towns I ever saw. Above seventy new houses were built in it last year, and

it is likely to increase in inhabitants every day. It is rightly
called Philadelphia, *i.e.* brotherly love; for by the charter all are
permitted to worship God their own way, without being
branded as schismatics, dissenters, or disturbers of the established
constitution. The Quakers have the pre-eminence in the government. The Assembly is made up of them, with the exception
of about four, which prevents all preparations for martial defence, it being one of their principles not to fight at all. Much
of the simplicity of dress and manners, which may be observed
among the inhabitants, I think is, in a great measure, owing to
them. I saw less of the pride of life in Pennsylvania than elsewhere. But it has happened to them, as it will to all other religious societies, when they flourish and have the upper-hand. I
mean that many, for profit's sake, have been known to dissemble
with them. I fear numbers amongst them, as amongst us, can
give no other reason why they are Quakers, than that their
fathers were so before them. I say this, because I find little of
Divine Power stirring amongst them; and most of them are too
stiff and rigid about external things, I was credibly informed.
One of their own preachers warned them lately of their back-
sliding, and told them, that without a reformation, God would
remove the candlestick from them, and work no more by their
hands. In the city of Philadelphia they have two large meeting-
houses, where they assemble frequently together; and, all things
considered, are the most regular society of men I have seen or
heard of. Besides this, there are Baptist and Presbyterian meetings. I had the pleasure of conversing with the ministers of both;
and found there were some in their congregations, particularly
in the Baptist, who loved the Lord Jesus in sincerity. The
Church of England is at a low ebb in the province in general,
and in Philadelphia in particular. In all places that I passed
through, the Presbyterians and Quakers had larger congregations than any of our missionaries; and we may guess that the
love of many of the Church of England in Philadelphia must
have waxed cold, for the church, which was begun, if I mistake
not, some years ago, is now far from being finished within.

Many of late, however, have been convinced what true Christianity is; and I hope a church of Jesus Christ will, ere long, be selected out of the members of our own communion.

The little time I was in New York would not permit me to make as many observations of the situation of affairs of religion in the province, as otherwise I might have done. A great complaint was made to me by some of the most serious inhabitants of it, that it was a very secure place, and that a work of God had never been carried on in it, since its first settlement. The heads of the Church of England seemed resolved to shut out the Kingdom of God from amongst them; but our Lord Jesus has been pleased to get Himself the victory; for though I was mostly opposed in New York, yet, if I may judge of what I saw myself, and have heard since my departure, as much, if not more good has been done there, than in any other place, in so short a time. In Maryland religion seems to be at a very low ebb. There are Roman Catholics in some parts, four congregations of Presbyterians, and a few Quakers; but by far the greatest part call themselves of the Church of England, which might, no doubt, greatly flourish were her ministers found faithful. But the Government, I fear, spoils them by giving them too much tobacco; for some, I hear, have thirty thousand, others fifty thousand, and others sixty thousand pounds of tobacco per annum. It is gathered by the High Sheriff of the County, and every person taxable is obliged to pay forty pounds of tobacco yearly to the ministers, though great numbers never hear or see them. In Virginia matters are not so bad. The ministers' stipends are not so large; the Commissary seems to have more power, and to exercise more discipline; but almost all are quite settled upon their lees. In Virginia, there are no Dissenters from the Established Church, except one or two meetings of Quakers. The importation of so many negroes and convicts is one great reason why there is so little religion to be seen; but the main cause of irreligion, bothin Virgina and Maryland, I take to be their not incorporating into towns: for hereby people living at a distance from the church, are apt to make every little thing serve as an

excuse to keep them from public worship. Whilst in this condition, religious societies cannot well be settled, and without con-
trol, wicked men may more easily revel and get drunk. Ministers, had they a will, cannot visit from house to house; and,
what is as bad as anything, schools for the education of children
cannot be so conveniently erected when the houses are so far
apart. The greatest probability of doing good in Virginia is
among the Scots-Irish, who have lately settled in the mountain-
ous parts of that province. They raise little or no tobacco, but
things that are useful for common life. I hear the Governor has
given leave for a minister of their own religious persuasion, to
come whenever he can be procured.

In North Carolina there is scarcely so much as the form of
religion. Two churches were begun, some time since, but neither is finished. There are several dancing-masters, but scarcely
one regular settled minister; so that in most places they have
readers, who read a sermon every Sunday to the people, for
which they pay five shillings a quarter of their currency, which
is ten shillings *sterling* for one. However, the Governor, I hear,
has made proposals to the Society for Propagating the Gospel
in Foreign Parts, to send missionaries. But I should rather that
people had no minister than such as are generally sent over; and
I cannot see the charity of contributing towards sending out
missionaries, unless greater care be taken in the choice of those
who are sent. All the accounts most of them have given for
some time is, that they have baptised so many, and that so many
have received the Sacrament; and, upon the whole, if it be asked
why there is so little religion in the Church of England, it may
be answered, the missionaries, who, for the most part, lead very
bad examples. In South Carolina they have many ministers, both
of our own and other persuasions; but I hear of no stirring
among the dry bones. Mr. Garden, the present Commissary, is
strict in the outward discipline of the Church. And now I
am come to Georgia, what shall I say? Many of the inhabitants
have left it since we were here last; but I hope blessings are in
reserve. Oh, that all who remain would acquaint themselves

with God, and be at peace with Him; then would they be more than conquerors over all their enemies.

Thus have I put down a few thoughts that have occurred to my mind. May God enlighten me where I am in the dark, correct me wherever I am wrong, and bless this further account of His dealings with me to all who shall read it. Amen.

An indigenous American tradition of revival did exist before 1740, especially in New England. Puritans enjoyed its own awakenings, partly through the ritual of reaffirming the covenants upon which the churches were founded. Begun during the crisis period of King Philip's War, this "communal owning of the covenant" produced considerable results in many communities, as the following letters from Samuel Danforth of Taunton, Massachusetts, attest.

SAMUEL HOPKINS EMERY
The Ministry of Taunton, with Incidental Notices of Other Professions.
Boston, 1853, pp. 257–260

"Covenant for Reformation, first engaged in the year 1676, and a second time renewed by the Inhabitants of Taunton, March 1, 1704–5."

We the inhabitants of Taunton, having a sense of the great displeasure of GOD against this whole land by stirring up the Heathen against us, and sending many other calamities upon us, Knowing that our Sins are the procuring cause of all these troubles, Do enter into solemn engagement (the LORD helping us by His grace, for of ourselves we have no sufficiency) to endeavour according to our several capacities, that there may be a real amendment and reformation in ourselves and those on whom we may have an influence, of those sins which are judged to have great influence in all the troubles of the land, such as general barrenness under the means of Grace, Neglect and contempt of the Gospel, Neutrality in Religion, Profanation of GOD'S holy Sabbath, indecent behaviour in the public worship

of GOD. Decay of the power of Godliness, Contempt of the
Magistracy and Ministry, Pride, Covetousness, Unrighteousness,
Profaneness, Incorrigibleness under the Word of GOD, and
under His rod, Abuse of GOD'S Mercies by Intemperance and
other fruits of the flesh: Also, Idleness, neglect of Family
Prayer, Unnecessary frequenting houses of Public Entertainment, Promise breaking and walking with Slanderers and reproachers of one another.

Acknowledging and Judging ourselves before the Lord that
we have been any way accessory by participation or commission
to any of these or other prevailing Sins of the Age and place
wherein we live, beseeching the Lord to give us sincere repentance and remission of all our sins through the Blood of
Christ, Do now Engage by GOD'S help to endeavour a suppression of open vice in ourselves and others, according to our
capacities, and that our houses shall not be houses of resort for
unlawful tippling or other disorders, And that the true Worship
of GOD as practised by His people and owned of GOD in
this Wilderness shall be upheld and maintained, and all within
our families made subject to good order and government, Beseeching the LORD to enable us to keep that which is gone out
of our mouth this day, that He may be our GOD, and may
give us a place in His Tabernacle, and may do good to us and
our Land.

Taunton, Feb. 20th, 1704–5.

SIR: —

We are much encouraged by an unusual & amazing Impression, made by God's Spirit on all sorts among us, especially on
the young men & women. Its almost incredible how many visit
me with discoveries of the extreme distress of mind they are
in about their Spiritual condition. And the young Men instead
of their merry meetings are now forming themselves into regular meetings for Prayer, repetition of Sermons, signing the same
order, which I obtained some years ago a copy of from the
Young Mens Meeting in the north of Boston. Some awful

Deaths & Amazing Providences have concur'd with the word preached to this good effect. The profanest among us seemed startled at the sudden change upon the rising generation. We need much prayer, that these Strivings of the Spirit may have a saving issue & effect. Our family meetings are more and more frequented. And two more family meetings setting up at two remote corners of our large Town, where we dispaired of seeing any. Our last Society which was yesterday had almost nothing to do, only to express their joy to each other, that the disorderly concourse of youth was now over. We are both, Church & all Inhabitants to renew the covenant for reformation this Week, which this people made with God the last Philip Indian War. We agreed to turn our next Society Meeting into a fast also, for special reasons; one of which was that we find prayer our best weapon to reform vice, & the Devils kingdom cant stand before it; also as worldly men, when they find the world comes hovering in upon them, will pull the harder for it; which should make us pray more earnestly & fervently: having had encouragement so far, that when we can do nothing else but stretch our withered hands in Gods work, Yet even doing of that shall not be in vain. Some Remarkables in the progress of our reformation work, I shall not commit to writing, at present; but if common fame do not bring them to you, shall reserve them to be discovered by word of mouth. The Lord be with you all, Amen.

Yours intirely, S. D.

Taunton, March 5th, 1704–5.

SIR: —

It was a most comfortable Day, the first of March, when we renewed the Reformation Covenant, of which I suppose you have a Copy by you already; only we added an engagement to reform idleness, unnecessary frequenting Houses of Public entertainment, irreverant behaviour in public Worship, Neglect of family prayer, Promise breaking & walking with slanderers, & Reproachers of others & that we should all in our families be

subject to good orders & Governments. It was read to the
brethren & sisters in the forenoon, they standing up as an outward sign of their inward consent to the rest of the inhabitants.
In the afternoon, they standing up also when it was read, &
then every one that stood up, brought his name ready writ in a
paper & put it into the box that it might be put on Church
Record. The forenoon text was, Hebrews 12:4, about resist-
ing and striving against Sin, the common enemy of us all. The
afternoon text was, 2 Chron. 29:10. We give liberty to all men
& women kind, from sixteen years old & upwards to act with us:
& had three Hundred Names given in to list under Christ against
the sins of the times. The whole acted with such gravity & tears
of good affection, as would affect an heart of Stone. Parents
weeping with Joy seeing their children give their Names to
Christ. And we had several children of the church in Neighboring Towns who came & joined with us in it. We have a Hundred more that will yet bind themselves in the Covenant, that
were then detained from meeting. Let God have the glory.
Yesterday fourteen were propounded to the Church, some for
full Communion, others for Baptism, being adult Persons. All
this calls for Prayer & humble walking with God, & hope in
his mercy.

Yours, S. D.

Taunton, March 20th, 1704–5.

SIR: —

I have now yours, and have sent you two Letters this
week. I have little to add and no time to Enlarge, but my time
is spent in daily discourse with the young People, Visiting me
with their doubts, fears & Agonies. Religion flourishes to
Amazement and Admiration, that so we should be at once
touched with Soul affliction, and this in all corners of the place,
and that our late conversions should be attended with more than
usual degrees of horror, and Satan permitted to wrestle with
them by Extraordinary temptations and assaults and hours of
Darkness. But I hope the deeper the wound the more sound

may be the cure. I have little time to think of worldly matters, scarce time to study sermons as I used to do. But find God can bless mean preparations when ever He pleases, that such shall be most cryed up and Commended which I have had scarce time to methodise. I think some times that the time of the pouring out of the Spirit upon all Flesh may be at the Door. Lets be earnest in prayer that Christ's Kingdom may come, and that being an Instrument of good to others, I may not be myself cast away.

Yours, S. D.

Still another series of revivals were produced in Northampton, Massachusetts, through the activities of Solomon Stoddard and his grandson, Jonathan Edwards. The Northampton "harvests," unlike others in America, received international publicity in the "Faithful Narrative of the Surprising Work of God" written by Edwards and published in 1737. Edwards' revivals were no more than isolated forerunners of the general catharsis which would strike America in 1740, but his description and analysis of events in Northampton were classic. If it did nothing else, the "Faithful Narrative" produced the vocabulary employed by all subsequent observers of the phenomenon of revivalism.

JONATHAN EDWARDS
The Works of President Edwards in Eight Volumes.
London, 1817, III, pp. 9–23

A GENERAL INTRODUCTORY STATEMENT

The people of the country, in general, I suppose, are as sober, orderly, and good sort of people, as in any part of New England; and I believe they have been preserved the freest by far of any part of the country, from *error*, and variety of *sects* and opinions. Our being so far *within* the land, at a distance from sea-ports, and in a corner of the country, has doubtles been *one reason* why we have not been so much corrupted with *vice;* as most other parts. But without question, the *religion* and good order of the county, and purity in *doctrine*, has, under God, been very much owing to the great abilities, and eminent piety, of my venerable and honoured grandfather Stoddard. I suppose we have been the freest of any part of the land from unhappy *divisions* and *quarrels* in our ecclesiastical and religious affairs, till the late lamentable *Springfield contention*.[1]

Being much seperated from other parts of the province, and having comparatively but little intercourse with them, we have always managed our ecclesiastical affairs within ourselves. It is the way in which the country, from its infancy, has gone on, by the practical agreement of all; and the way in which our peace and good order has hitherto been maintained.

The town of Northampton is of about 82 years standing, and has now about 200 families; which mostly dwell more *compactly* together than any town of such size in these parts of the country. This probably has been an occasion, that both our *corruptions* and *reformations* have been, from time to time, the more *swiftly* propagated from one to another through the town. Take the town in general, and so far as I can judge, they are as *rational* and *intelligent* a people as most I have been acquainted with. Many of them have been *noted* for religion; and, particularly remarkable for their distinct *knowledge* in things that relate to *heart* religion, and christian *experience*, and their great *regards* thereto.

I am the *third minister* who has been settled in the town. The Rev. Mr. Eleazer Mather, who was the *first*, was ordained in July, 1669. He was one whose heart was *much* in his work, and abundant in *labours* for the good of precious souls. He had the high esteem and great love of his people, and was blessed with no small *success*. The Rev. Mr. Stoddard who succeeded him, came first to the town the November after his death; but was not ordained till September 11, 1672, and died February 11, 1728–9. So that he continued in the work of the ministry here,

---

[1] The *Springfield* Contention relates to the settlement of a minister there, which occasioned too warm debates between some, both pastors and people, that were for it, and others that were against it, on account of their different apprehensions about his principles, and about some steps that were taken to procure his ordination.

from his first coming to town, near 60 years. And as he was eminent and *renowned* for his gifts and grace; so he was blessed, from the beginning, with *extraordinary success* in his ministry, in the conversion of many souls. He had *five harvests*, as he called them. The *first* was about 57 years ago; the *second* about 53; the *third* about 40; the *fourth* about 24; the *fifth* and last about 18 years ago. *Some* of these times were much more remarkable than others, and the ingathering of souls more plentiful. Those about 53, and 40, and 24 years ago, were much greater than either the *first* or the *last:* but in *each* of them, I have heard my grandfather say, the greater part of the *young* people in the town, seemed to be mainly concerned for their eternal salvation.

After the *last* of these, came a far more degenerate time, (at least among the young people) I suppose, than ever before. Mr. Stoddard, indeed, had the comfort, before he died, of seeing a time where there were no small appearances of a divine work among some, and a considerable *ingathering* of souls, even after I was settled with him in the *ministry*, which was about *two* years before his death; and I have reason to *bless God* for the great advantage I had by it. In these *two* years there were nearly *twenty* that Mr. Stoddard hoped to be savingly converted; but there was nothing of any general awakening. The greater part seemed to be at that time very insensible of the things of religion, and engaged in other cares and pursuits. Just after my grandfather's death, it seemed to be a time of extraordinary dulness in religion. *Licentiousness* for some years greatly prevailed among the *youth* of the town; they were many of them very much addicted to *nightwalking*, and frequenting the *tavern*, and *lewd* practices, wherein some, by their example, exceedingly corrupted others. It was their manner very frequently to get together, in conventions of both *sexes*, for mirth and jollity, which they called *frolicks;* and they would often spend the greater part of the *night* in them, without regard to any *order* in the families they belonged to: and indeed *family government* did too much fail in the town. It was become very customary with many of our young people to be *indecent* in their carriage at *meeting*, which doubtless would not have prevailed in such a degree, had it not been that my *grand-father* through his *great age*, (though he retained his *powers* surprisingly to the *last*) was not so able to *observe* them. There had also long prevailed in the town a spirit of contention between *two parties*, into which they had for many years been *divided;* by which they maintained a *jealousy* one of the other, and were prepared to *oppose* one another in all public affairs.

But in *two* or *three* years after Mr. Stoddard's death, there began to be a sensible amendment of these evils. The *young people* shewed more of a disposition to hearken to counsel and by degrees left off their *frolicks;* they grew observably more *decent* in their attendance on the public worship, and there were more who manifested a *religious concern* than there used to be.

At the latter end of the year 1733, there appeared a very unusual flexibleness, and yielding to advice, in our young people. It had been too long their manner to make the *evening after the sabbath*,[2] and after our public *lecture*, to be especially the times of their *mirth*, and company-keeping. But a *sermon* was now preached on the sabbath before the *lecture*, to shew the *evil tendency* of the practice, and to persuade them to reform it; and it was urged on *heads of families* that it should be a thing *agreed* upon among them, to govern their families, and keep their children at home, at these times. It was also more *privately* moved, that they should meet together the next day, in their several neighbourhoods, to know each other's minds; which was accordingly done, and the *motion* complied with throughout the town. But *parents* found little or no occasion for the exercise of government in the case. The *young people* declared themselves *convinced* by what they had heard from

---

[2] It must be noted, that it has never been our manner, to observe the *evening* that *follows* the sabbath; but that which *precedes* it, as part of the holy time.

the *pulpit*, and were willing of themselves to comply with the counsel that had been given: and it was *immediately*, and, I suppose almost *universally* complied with; and there was a thorough *reformation* of these disorders thenceforward, which has continued ever since.

Presently after this, there began to appear a *remarkable religious concern* at a little village belonging to the congregation called Pascommuck, where a few families were settled, at about three miles distance from the main body of the town. At this place, a number of persons seemed to be savingly wrought upon. In the April following, *Anno* 1734, there happened a *sudden and awful death of a young man* in the bloom of his youth; who being violently seized with *pleurisy*, and taken immediately very *delirious*, died in about *two days;* which (together with what was preached publicly on that occasion) *much affected* many young people. This was followed with another death of a young married woman, who had been considerably *exercised* in mind, about the salvation of her *soul*, before she was ill, and was in great *distress*, in the beginning of her illness; but seemed to have *satisfying evidences* of God's saving *mercy* to her, before her death; so that she died very full of *comfort*, in a most earnest and moving manner *warning*, and counselling others. This seemed to *contribute* to render solemn the spirits of many young persons; and there began evidently to appear more of a *religious concern* on people's minds.

In the fall of the year I proposed it to the *young people*, that they should agree among themselves to spend the *evenings after lectures* in *social* religion, and to that end divide themselves into several companies to meet in various parts of the town; which was accordingly done, and those *meetings* have been since continued, and the *example* imitated by *elder* people. This was followed with the death of an *elderly* person, which was attended with many *unusual* circumstances, by which many were much moved and affected.

About this time began the great *noise*, in this part of the country, about *Arminianism*, which seemed to appear with a very *threatening* aspect upon the interest of religion here. The friends of vital piety trembled for fear of the issue; but it seemed, contrary to their fear, strongly to be *over-ruled* for the promoting of religion. Many who looked on themselves as in a *Christless* condition, seemed to be awakened by it, with fear that God was about to withdraw from the land, and that we should be given up to *heterodoxy* and corrupt principles; and that then their *opportunity* for obtaining salvation would be past. Many who were brought a little to *doubt* about the *truth* of the *doctrines* they had hitherto been taught, seemed to have a kind of trembling *fear* with their doubts, lest they should be led into *by-paths*, to their eternal undoing; and they seemed, with much concern and engagedness of mind, to enquire what was indeed the way in which they must come to be accepted with God. There were some things said *publicly* on that occasion, concerning *justification by faith alone.*

Although great *fault* was found with *meddling* with the *controversy* in the pulpit, by such a person, and at that time — and though it was ridiculed by many *elsewhere* — yet it proved a word spoken in season here; and was most evidently attended with a very remarkable *blessing* of heaven to the souls of the people in this town. They received thence a general satisfaction, with respect to the main thing in question, which they had been in trembling doubts and concern about; and their minds were engaged the more earnestly to seek that they might come to be accepted of God, and saved in the way of the gospel, which had been made evident to them to be the true and only way. And *then* it was, in the latter part of *December, that the Spirit of God* began extraordinarily to set in, and *wonderfully* to work amongst us; and there were, very *suddenly*, one after another, five or six persons, who were to all appearance savingly converted, and some of them wrought upon in a very remarkable manner.

Particularly, I was surprised with the relation of a *young woman*, who had been one of the greatest company-keepers in the whole town. When she came to me, I had never heard that she was become in any wise serious, but by the conversation I then had with her, it appeared to me, that what she gave an account of, was a glorious work of God's infinite power and sovereign grace; and that God had given her a *new* heart, truly broken and sanctified. I could not then doubt of it, and have seen much in my acquaintance with her since to confirm it.

Though the work was *glorious*, yet I was filled with concern about the *effect* it might have upon others. I was ready to conclude, (though too rashly) that some would be *hardened* by it, in carelessness and looseness of life; and would take occasion from it to open their mouths in *reproaches* of religion. But the *event* was the *reverse*, to a wonderful degree. God made it, I suppose, the *greatest occasion of awakening* to others, of any thing that ever came to pass in the town. I have had abundant opportunity to know the effect it had, by my private conversation with many. The news of it seemed to be almost like a *flash of lightning*, upon the hearts of young people, all over the town, and upon many others. Those persons amongst us, who used to be *farthest* from seriousness, and that I most feared would make an ill improvement of it, seemed greatly to be *awakened* with it. Many went to talk with her, concerning what she had met with; and what appeared in her seemed to be to the satisfaction of all that did so.

Presently upon this, a great and earnest concern about the great things of religion, and the eternal world, became *universal* in all parts of the town, and among persons of all degrees, and all ages. The noise amongst the *dry bones* waxed louder and louder; all other talk but about spiritual and eternal things, was soon thrown by; all the conversation, in all companies and upon all occasions, was upon these things only, unless so much as was necessary for people carrying on their ordinary secular business. Other discourse than of the things of religion, would scarcely be tolerated in any company. The minds of people were wonderfully taken off from the *world*, it was treated amongst us as a thing of very little consequence. They seemed to follow their worldly business, more as a part of their duty, than from any disposition they had to it; the *temptation* now seemed to lie on that hand, to *neglect* worldly affairs too much, and to spend too much time in the immediate exercise of religion. This exceedingly misrepresented by reports that were spread in distant parts of the land, as though the people here had wholly thrown by all worldly business, and betook themselves entirely to reading and praying, and such like religious exercises.

But although people did not ordinarily neglect their worldly business; yet *Religion* was with all sorts the great concern, and the *world* was a thing only by the bye. The only thing in their view was to get the kingdom of heaven, and every one appeared pressing into it. The engagedness of their hearts in this great concern could not be *hid*, it appeared in their very *countenances*. It then was a dreadful thing amongst us to lie out of Christ, in danger every day of dropping into hell; and what persons minds were intent upon was to *escape for their lives*, and to *fly from the wrath to come*. All would eagerly lay hold of opportunities for their souls; and were wont very often to meet together in private houses, for religious purposes: and such meetings when appointed were greatly thronged.

There was scarcely a single person in the town, old or young, left unconcerned about the great things of the eternal world. Those who were wont to be the vainest, and loosest; and those who had been most disposed to think, and speak slightly of vital and experimental religion, were now generally subject to great awakenings. And the work of *conversion* was carried on in a most *astonishing* manner, and increased more and more; souls did as it were come by flocks to Jesus Christ. From day to day, for many months together, might be seen evident instances of sinners brought *out of darkness into marvellous light,* and delivered *out of an horrible pit, and from the miry clay, and set upon a rock* with a *new song of praise to God in their mouths.*

This work of God, as it was carried on, and the number of true saints multiplied, soon made a glorious alteration in the town; so that in the spring and summer following, *Anno* 1735, the town seemed to be full of the presence of God: it never was so full of *love*, nor of *joy*, and yet so full of distress, as it was then. There were remarkable tokens of God's presence in almost every house. It was a time of joy in *families* on account of salvation being brought unto them; *parents* rejoicing over their children as new born, and *husbands* over their wives, and *wives* over their husbands. *The goings of God* were then *seen in his sanctuary*, God's *day* was a *delight*, and his *tabernacles* were *amiable*. Our public assemblies were then beautiful; the congregation was *alive* in God's service, every one earnestly intent on the public worship, every *hearer* eager to drink in the words of the *minister* as they came from his mouth; the assembly in general were, from time to time, *in tears* while the word was preached; *some* weeping with sorrow and distress, *others* with joy and love, *others* with pity and concern for the souls of their neighbours.

Our public *praises* were then greatly enlivened; God was then served in our *psalmody*, in some measure, in the *beauty of holiness*. It has been observable, that there has been scarce *any part* of divine worship, wherein good men amongst us have had *grace so drawn forth*, and their hearts *so lifted up* in the ways of God, as *in singing* his praises. Our congregation excelled all that ever I knew in the *external* part of the duty before, the men generally carrying regularly, and well, *three parts of music*, and the *women* a part by themselves; but now they were evidently wont to sing with *unusual elevation* of heart and voice, which made the duty pleasant indeed.

In all *companies*, on *other* days, on whatever *occasions* persons met together, *Christ* was to be heard of, and seen in the midst of them. Our *young people*, when they met, were wont to spend the time in talking of the *excellency* and dying *love* of JESUS CHRIST, the glory of the way of *salvation*, the wonderful, free, and sovereign grace of God, his glorious work in the *conversion* of a soul, the *truth* and certainty of the great things of

God's word, the sweetness of the views of his *perfections, &c.*
And even at *weddings*, which formerly were mere occasions of
mirth and jollity, there was now no discourse of any thing but
religion, and no appearance of any but *spiritual mirth*. Those
amongst us who had been *formerly converted*, were greatly enlivened, and renewed with fresh and extraordinary incomes of
the spirit of God; though some much more than others, *according to the measure of the gift of Christ.* Many who before had
laboured under *difficulties* about their own state, had now their
doubts removed by more satisfying experience, and more clear
discoveries of God's love.

When this work first appeared, and was so extraordinarily
carried on amongst *us* in the winter, *others* round about us
seemed not to know what to make of it. Many scoffed at and
ridiculed it; and some compared what we called conversion,
to certain *distempers*. But it was very observable of many, who
occasionally came amongst us from abroad with disregardful
hearts, that what they saw here cured them of such a temper of
mind. *Strangers* were generally surprised to find things so much
beyond what they had heard, and were wont to tell others that
the state of the town could not be conceived of by those who
had not seen it. The notice that was taken of it by the people
who came to town on occasion of the *court* that sat here in the
beginning of March, was very observable. And those who
came from the neighbourhood to our public *lectures*, were for
the most part remarkably affected. Many who came to town,
on one occasion or other, had their consciences smitten, and
awakened; and went home with wounded hearts, and with those
impressions that never wore off till they had hopefully a saving
issue; and those who before had serious thoughts, had their
awakenings and convictions greatly increased. There were
many instances of persons who came from abroad on visits, or
on business, who had not been long here before, to all appearance, they were savingly wrought upon; and partook of that
shower of divine blessing which God rained down here, and

went home rejoicing; till at length the *same work* began evidently to appear and prevail in several other towns in the *county*.

In the month of March, the people in *South Hadley* began to be seized with deep concern about the things of religion; which very soon became universal. The work of God has been very wonderful *there;* not much, if any thing, short of what it has been here, in proportion to the size of the place. About the same time, it began to break forth in the west part of *Suffield*, (where it also has been very great) and it soon spread into all parts of the town. It next appeared at *Sunderland,* and soon overspread the town; and I believe was, for a season, not less remarkable than it was here. About the same time it began to appear in a part of *Deerfield,* called *Green River,* and afterwards filled the town, and there has been a *glorious* work there. It began also to be manifest, in the south part of *Hatfield,* in a place called the *Hill,* and the *whole town,* in the second week in April, seemed to be seized, as it were at once, with concern about the things of religion; and the work of God has been *great* there. There has been also a very general awakening at *West-Springfield,* and *Long Meadow;* and in *Enfield* there was for a time a pretty general concern amongst some who before had been very loose persons. About the same time that this appeared at *Enfield,* the Rev. Mr. Bull, of *Westfield,* informed me, that there had been a great alteration *there,* and that more had been done in *one week,* than in *seven years* before. Something of this work likewise appeared in the first precinct in *Springfield,* principally in the north and south extremes of the parish. And in *Hadley* old town, there gradually appeared so much of a work of God on souls, as at another time would have been thought worthy of much notice. For a *short* time there was also a very great and general concern, of the like nature, at *Northfield.* And wherever this concern appeared, it seemed not to be *in vain:* but in every place God brought saving blessings with him, and his *word* attended with his *spirit* (as we have all reason to think) returned *not void*. It might well be said at that time, in all parts of the county, *who are these that fly as a cloud, and as doves to their windows?*

As what *other* towns heard of and found in this, was a great means of awakening *them;* so *our* hearing of such a swift, and extraordinary propagation, and extent of this work, did doubtless for a time serve to uphold the work amongst us. The continual news kept alive the talk of religion, and did greatly quicken and rejoice the hearts of God's people, and much awakened those who looked on themselves as still *left behind*, and made them the more earnest that they also might *share* in the great blessings that others had obtained.

This remarkable *pouring out of the Spirit of God*, which thus extended from one end to the other of this county, was not confined to it, but many places in Connecticut have partaken in the same mercy. For instance, the first parish in Windsor, under the pastoral care of the Rev. Mr. Marsh, was thus blest about the same time as we in Northampton, while we had *no knowledge* of each other's circumstances. There has been a very great ingathering of souls to *Christ* in that place, and something considerable of the same work begun afterwards in East Windsor, my honoured father's parish, which has *in times past* been a place favoured with mercies of this nature, *above any* on this western side of New England, excepting Northampton; there having been *four*, or *five* seasons of the *pouring out of the spirit* to the *general* awakening of the people there, since my father's settlement amongst them.

There was also the *last* spring and summer a wonderful work of God carried on at *Coventry*, under the ministry of the Rev. Mr. Meacham. I had opportunity to converse with some Coventry people, who gave me a very remarkable account of the surprising *change* that appeared in the most rude and vicious persons there. The like was also very great at the same time in a part of Lebanon, called the *Crank*, where the Rev. Mr. Wheelock, a young gentleman, is lately settled: and there has been much of the same at Durham, under the ministry of the Rev. Mr. Chauncey; and to appearance no small ingathering of souls there. Likewise amongst many of the young people in the first precinct in *Stratford*, under the ministry of the Rev. Mr. Gould; where the work was much promoted by the remarkable conversion of a young woman who had been a great company-keeper, as it was here.

Something of this work appeared in several other *towns* in those parts, as I was informed when I was there, the last *fall*. And we have since been acquainted with something very remarkable of this nature at another parish in Stratford, called *Ripton*, under the pastoral care of the Rev. Mr. Mills. There was a considerable revival of religion last summer at *Newhaven* old town, as I was once and again informed by the Rev. Mr. Noyes, the minister there, and by others: and by a letter which I very lately received from Mr. Noyes, and also by information we have had other ways. This flourishing of religion still continues, and has lately much increased. Mr. Noyes writes, that *many this summer have been added to the church*, and particularly mentions several young persons that belong to the principal families of that town.

There has been a degree of the same work at a part of *Guildford;* and very considerable at *Mansfield*, under the ministry of the Rev. Mr. Eleazar Williams; and an unusual religious concern at *Tolland;* and something of it at *Hebron*, and *Bolton*. There was also no small effusion of the spirit of God in the north parish in *Preston*, in the eastern part of Connecticut, of which I was informed, and saw something, when I was the last autumn at the house, and in the congregation of the Rev. Mr. Lord, the minister there; who, with the Rev. Mr. Owen, of Groton, came up hither in May, the last year, on purpose to see the work of God. Having heard various and contradictory accounts of it, they were careful when here to satisfy themselves; and to that end particularly conversed with many of our people; which they declared to be entirely to their satisfaction;

and that the *one half had not been told them*, nor could be told them. Mr. Lord told me that, when he got home, he informed his congregation of what he had seen, and that they were greatly affected with it; and that it proved the beginning of the same work amongst them, which prevailed till there was a *general* awakening, and many instances of persons, who seemed to be remarkably converted. I also have lately heard that there has been something of the same work at *Woodbury*.

But this shower of divine blessing has been yet more *extensive:* there was no small degree of it in some parts of the *Jerseys;* as I was informed when I was at New York, (in a long journey I took at that time of the year for my health) by some people of the Jerseys, whom I saw. Especially the Rev. William Tennent, a minister who seemed to have such things much at heart, told me of a very great awakening of many in a place called the *Mountains,* under the ministry of one Mr. Cross; and of a very considerable revival of religion in another place under the ministry of his brother the Rev. Gilbert Tennent; and also at another place, under the ministry of a very pious young gentleman, a Dutch minister, whose name as I remember was Freelinghousa.

This seems to have been a very *extraordinary* dispensation of providence; God has in many respects gone out of, and much beyond his usual, and *ordinary way.* The work in this town, and some others about us, has been extraordinary on account of the *universality* of it, affecting all sorts, sober and vicious, high and low, rich and poor, wise and unwise. It reached the most considerable families and persons, to all appearance, as much as others. In former stirrings of this nature, the bulk of the *young* people have been greatly affected; but *old men* and *little children* have been so now. Many of the *last* have, of their own accord, formed themselves into *religious societies,* in different parts of the town. A loose careless person could scarcely be found in the whole neighbourhood; and if there was *any one* that seemed to remain senseless or unconcerned, it would be spoken of as a *strange* thing.

This dispensation has also appeared very extraordinary in the *numbers* of those on whom we have reason to hope it has had a saving effect. We have about *six hundred and twenty communicants*, which include almost all our adult persons. The church was very *large* before; but persons never *thronged* into it, as they did in the late extraordinary time. — Our *sacraments* are eight weeks asunder, and I received into our communion about a *hundred* before one sacrament, *fourscore* of them at one time, whose appearance, when they presented themselves together to make an open explicit *profession* of christianity, was very affecting to the congregation. I took in near *sixty* before the next sacrament day: and I had very sufficient evidence of the conversion of their souls, through divine grace, though it is not the custom here, as it is in many other churches in this country, to make a credible relation of their inward experiences the ground of admission to the Lord's Supper.

I am far from pretending to be able to determine how many have lately been the subjects of such mercy; but if I may be allowed to declare any thing that appears to me probable in a thing of this nature, I hope that more than 300 souls were savingly brought home to Christ, in this town, in the space of half a year, and about the same number of males as females. By what I have heard Mr. Stoddard say, this was far from what has been usual in years past; for he observed that in his time, many more women were converted than men. Those of our young people who are on other accounts most considerable, are mostly, as I hope, truly pious, and leading persons in the ways of religion. Those who were formerly looser young persons, are generally, to all appearance, become true lovers of God and Christ, and spiritual in their dispositions. I hope that by far the greater part of persons in this town, above sixteen years of age, are such as have the saving knowledge of Jesus Christ. By what I have heard I suppose it is so in some other places; particularly at *Sunderland* and *South Hadley*.

This has also appeared to be a very extraordinary dispensation, in that the spirit of God has so much extended not only his *awakening*, but *regenerating* influences, both to *elderly* persons, and also those who are *very young*. It has been heretofore rarely heard of, that *any* were converted past middle age; but now we have the same ground to think, that *many such* have at this time been savingly changed, as that *others* have been so in more early years. I suppose there were upwards of *fifty* persons converted in this town above forty years of age; more than *twenty* of them above fifty; about *ten* of them above sixty; and *two* of them above seventy years of age.

It has heretofore been looked on as a strange thing, when any have seemed to be savingly wrought upon, and remarkably changed in their *childhood*. But now, I suppose, near *thirty* were, to appearance, savingly wrought upon, between ten and fourteen years of age; *two* between nine and ten, and *one* of about four years of age; and because I suppose this last will be with most difficulty believed, I will hereafter give a particular account of it. The influences of God's Holy Spirit have also been very remarkable on children in some *other* places; particularly at *Sunderland, South Hadley,* and the west part of *Suffield.* There are several *families* in this town who are *all* hopefully pious. Yea, there are several numerous families, in which, I think, we have reason to hope that all the children are truly godly, and most of them lately become so. There are very few *houses* in the whole town, into which salvation has not lately come, in one or more instances. There are several *negroes,* who from what was seen in them then, and what is discernable in them since, appear to have been truly born again in the late remarkable season.

God has also seemed to have gone out of his usual way, in the *quickness* of his work, and the swift progress his Spirit has made in his operations on the hearts of many. It is wonderful that persons should be so *suddenly,* and yet so *greatly* changed. Many have been taken from a loose and careless way of living, and seized with strong convictions of their guilt and misery, and in a very little time old things have passed away, and all things have become new with them.

God's work has also appeared very extraordinary in the *degrees* of his influences; in the degrees both of *awakening* and conviction, and also of *saving light, love,* and *joy,* that many have experienced. It has also been very extraordinary in the *extent* of it, and its being so swiftly propagated from town to town. In former times of the pouring out of the Spirit of God on this town, though in some of them it was very remarkable, it reached no further than, the neighbouring towns all around continued unmoved.

This work seemed to be at its greatest height in this town, in the former part of the spring, in March and April. At that time, God's work in the conversion of souls was carried on amongst us in so wonderful a manner, that, so far as I can judge, it appears to have been at the rate, at least, of four persons in a day; or near thirty in a week, take one with another, for five or six weeks together. When God in so remarkable a manner took the work into his own hands, there was as much done in a *day or two* as at ordinary times, with all endeavours that men can use, and with such a blessing as we commonly have, is done in a *year.*

I am very sensible how apt many would be, if they should see the account I have here given, presently to think with themselves that I am very fond of making a great many converts, and of magnifying the matter; and to think that, for want of judgment, I take every religious pang, and enthusiastic conceit, for saving conversion. I do not much wonder, if they should be apt to think so; and, for this reason, I have forborne to publish an account of this great work of God, though I have often been solicited. But having now a special call to give an account of it, upon mature consideration I thought it might not be beside my duty to declare this amazing work, as it appeared to me to be indeed divine, and to conceal no part of the glory of it; leaving it with God to take care of the credit of his own work, and running the venture of any censorious thoughts, which might be entertained of me to my disadvantage.

The American colonies in 1740 were experiencing a good many pressures and tensions which made large segments of the population uneasy. The following selections illustrate some of these forces. Josiah Cotton's enumeration of the trials and tribulations of life in New England in 1740 may suggest some of the motives that led that region to embrace revivalism in that year. A letter from Pennsylvania in 1738 presents a view of conditions in the Middle Colonies as seen by German immigrants. Lieutenant-Governor George Clark of New York offers explanations for an outbreak of deviant behavior in his colony in 1741.

JOSIAH COTTON

"Memoirs containing Some Account of the Predecessors, Relations, Posterity & Alliances (with some remarkable Occurrencies in the Life and Circumstances) of Josiah Cotton of Plymouth in New England, Esq. . . ."

Boston, Manuscript in Massachusetts Historical Society, 286–296

Plym'o Dies Jovis Janu'y 30. 1740/1

I have read of a certain Sect or sort of men that thought there were two principles from whence all things proceed, the one the author of good, the other of evil. But christianity informs us otherwise & better, that God alone is the author of the evil that we suffer as well as of the good that we enjoy, for shall we receive good at the hands of God, & which we dont deserve, & not evil which we do? The evil of sin merits the evil of punishment; & the Almighty as he is Judge & Gov'r of the world is obliged in Justice to punish moral evil with penal. The diseases of our bodies proceed from the distempers of our minds some of which diseases the nature & constitutions of men admits but one of the life of man. VIZ: the plague, smallpox & meazells, which last distemper came into our family about the middle of Janu'y last, our negro man Quominuh being first seized therewith, & then his son, a child about five years old, & then our youngest daughter, & eldest Granddaughter, all sick with it at the same time: and a great snow falling the 15th of January which lasted many weeks & rendered our case very difficult, having but little or no help but my wife & Sias but the author of our affliction carried us thro' it, tho the negro had a relapse, & was not well till about the beginning of march & what shall we render to the Lord for spairing our lives? That distemper run thro' the town very swiftly but proved favourable to a sinfull ill deserving people thro sovereign grace & mercy. Our Son Josiah belonged then to the Colledge, but was I think by a good providence detained at home, without whose help we had suffered much more than we did: & all the month of March was hindered by contrary winds from his return to Cambridge, so that he did not get there till the beginning of april, & then was fin'd or punish't 3 £ for absence; upon which occasion I wrote several letters to the President & the fellows, some passages whereof I shall transcribe: To the President I wrote, that he took a great deal of pains to obtain a passage walking near 40 times 4 miles a day in order thereunto, but Eolus not favouring him I wish Apollo may, & then add some news forreign to this affair, concerning a monstrous ly raised by an Indian to conceal some mischief he had done, a story ridiculous & incredible that Eight Spaniards had taken him & his house in the wood 4 miles from the salt water as if they sailed over the tops of the trees & landed safe a[t] Jo. Wainpums house howsoever it put this town into the utmost confusion upon the Lords day March the 30th but ended without blood. The story of 2 youngsters fooling & playing together viz: Eames & Morton, & the first runing a red hot Iron into the others throat & thereby killing him directly, was too true to make a jest of &c. I afterwards wrote a particular account of the occasion of my Sons tarrying so long at home to his Tutor Mr Joseph Mahen . . . & received an answer from him, with encouragement, that they would reconsider his fine, whereupon Josiah tarried at Cambridge till the last week in June at which time the Colledge broke up by reason of the throat distemper then prevailing in the town of which the Presidents Wife &c. died, & the Commencement was put off to the 27th of August, & the Schollars ordered to repair to the Colledge about that time, but considering that my Sons fine was not reconsidered, & he not sufficiently fitted up to go,

I detained him to go, & on the 6th of Sept'r sent him to Narra-
gansett to bring down Bille Dyre, which he happily accomplished on September 25 & blessed be God, who has thus answered our prayers & strenuous endeavours to rescue him from
rudeness, ignorance & Quakerism. He tarried at our house till
the 7th of Nov'r & then set sail for Boston, with his Uncle Sias,
where they arrived the same day, & the poor fatherless & Mother-
less child was well received of his great Uncle. Sias tarried there
& thereabouts till Dec'r 20th & then arrived home, I having left
him at his liberty either to tarry or come away from the Colledge, which last he chose, & what the event will be God only
knows. Oh that it may be the better, & not for the worse, &
that we may now have direction from Heaven, what course to
stear concerning him, & if this change of our designs may not
prove ruinous to him. In my writing to the President &c. I
hinted that reason & Justice were on my design, & that they
ought to prevail in all societies, & refered to several instances
wherein, those that had the powers relaxed the severity of penal
laws, which would make sad work in the world if moderation
were not used in the execution of them, & that no body ought
to be punished purely as an example, only to deter others from
taking too much, but that they were Gentlemen self sufficient
& not obliged to copy of precedents. I wrote this because his
Tutor promised to call at my house, but failed to be at the door
&c. That civility, good manners, & all things else in law &
Gospel had taken a different turn from what they had in the
last century, and that I could not but consider they had not
reconsidered the matter in Sept'r in as much as we ought to be
as speedy in doing Justice as injustice &c. The reason of my
labouring the matter so much was to prevent such proceedings
in the future, supposing no appeal, or remedy but was as bad
as the diseas, but all to no purpose, & so proceed to say we may
sing of judgment as well as mercy, mercy in receiving our
GrandChild & judgment perhaps in diverting the Education of
our Son & in the loss of our Negro man, who strangly & unexpectedly left us on the 29th of Octob'r & after lurcking about

the town 4 or 5 days went to Boston, altho pains have been
taken to get him here, yet remains abroad, and may we not read
our sin in our punishment? We have often deserted the service
of our heavenly benefactor, & no wonder he permits our Servants to wonder if he permits our [ ] only in this but in other
respects we may take notice of the divine goodness & severity.
Our Son in law Dyre thro' the mismanagement of his owner &
imployer one Cornet a Frenchman lost his whole Voyage to
Hispaniola (which was near 9 mo) & had like to have lost his
life with sickness, as several of his Company did, viz: young
Thomas Howland & his Brother Joseph, one of Capt'n Benj'n
Warrens Sons &c: Howsoever thro' divine Goodness Dyre at
length returned as it were with the skin of his Teeth, & has since
made a very quick & successful Voyage to Portugal — & our
Son Theophilus has also made 2 good voyages to Jamaica this
year. Oh that this sort of men were more gratefull to their
gracious preserver from the danger of the Seas & enemies. The
Spaniards have taken many of the English vessells this year,
some perhaps that sailed from hence: and to reveng the injuries
done upon us, a design has been formed in England of attacking
(as tis said) the Havanna a very strong & rich City upon Cuba
in the West Indies, for which purpose several Companies of
voluntiers were listed in America, & in this Province 5 Companies, one of which was commanded by Maj'r John Winslow
(Son of Col'o Winslow late Dec'd) formerly Clerk of our
Court, who strangely & unaccountably left his farm, his family,
his aged mother, & his business which was considerable, to ram-
ble abroad in the world upon such a dangerious Enterprise &c.
In my last years memoirs I mention the receipt of a letter from
Cous'n Cotton of the Isle of Wight & since I returned an answer
Dated March 25: 1740. . . . I inform him also of our danger
by a French War & the dangerous circumstances of our eclesias-
tical constitution for want of a decisive power & I cant forbear
informing him (upon giving occasion in his Letter from what
he had heard concerning us) that we are in this Countrey got
into very ill methods of Living, the getting of a mans living by

the sweat of his face (according to the original Curse) is too
much out of fashion. The Sea Swallows up the land, too many
Sailers, & too few Husbandmen; we don't love to labour in
bringing our land too by which means & an extravagance of living beyond ourselves we are forc'd to be beholden to other parts
for provision. Ireland for times for Butter, England for Cloath-
ing &c which carries off our Silver & leaves us nothing but Paper
money, the difficulties & damage whereof seem to be inextrica-
ble & insuperable. This year two several parcells of men undertook & ventured to put out vast sums of paper money viz: the
Merchants at Boston 120 Thousand pounds to be repaid in silver
or Gold at the end of 15 years & the Countrey men in conjunc-
tion with some at Boston to put out some Thousand pound
reconed 60000 £ of the old currant paper Bills to be paid in
again in 20 years in the produce of the countrey except Wooll
& Fish upon which two schemes it was observed by one that the
first will oppress the poor & the last the rich, the first chiefly
upon personal security, & the last upon land security, & therefore called the land security as the first is called silver scheme
which has the favour & countenance of the Government but
the land scheme is exceedingly frowned upon in the first place
before any of their money came out a proclamation came forth
to caution all from taking any of their money, & after it did get
out & many did & some did not receive it, 2 proclamations more
came forth from the Gov'r & Councill threatning all Civil &
military Officers with the displeasure of the Gov't displacing
if they incouraged the passing the land scheme money, in pur-
suan whereof several worthy men have been dismist from their
Civil & military posts: & since that a threatning order to discourage Tavern keepers from taking it, & directions to the
Justices not to license such as do, & what these things tend to,
God end in God only knows, *Deus avertat omen*, that it may
not end in a Storm that will overwhelm us all. I received an
order Jan'y 3d from the Gov'r & Councill to transmit a list of
all such persons names as had morgaged their estates or any part
thereof to the Society who have put forth notes of hand com-

monly called manifactures Bills which List I sent to the Secretary & had prepared in a seperate letter the following animadversions but did not send it viz; Sr. I am a little or rather not a little concerned at the aspect of the Times. The Countrey seem to have their hearts much set upon the Land scheme as that which will promot the manifactures of the Countrey, & as their last shift & only asylum to deliver them from extorting Rhode Islanders, designing hoarders & devouring usurers; & Merchants among ourselves who require silver for their Notes of hand, & take due care to prevent it out of the Countrey as fast as they can, & may it not be justly feared that the strong efforts to prevent this extraordinary scheme will have a contrary effect to what may be intended, & render the peccant humour more fervent & intense? *Nitimur in vetitium* people have suckt in with their mothers milk, & when they see otherwise good & worthy men displac'd because they cant see just as others do alas what will it come to? Thus far the Countrey talk, not considering that the thinning of officers & Tavernskeepers may be of publick use. For my own part I have been for many years an enemy to the multiplying nay the very being of paper money, but as long as Rhode Island take the liberty of pouring in such a floud upon us, & the Merchants make what & when they please I can see no end to it, only some faint glimmering hopes that these excessive emissions will so Glutt us that we shall have no future appetite to such a wretched medium or will otherwise procure a total suppression of it. I shall finish this as I did my last. Money, & the want of money will ruine me. There have been several storms this year in Oct'r, Nov'r, Dec'r & this month, which have done much damage to bridges Dams & Vessells: many wrecks &c, much & many Snow & very hard & cold weather even to this day. . . . Our Bay has been so filled with Ice that many have walked upon it from Plymouth to Duxborough, that several vessells have not been able to reach the shore for several weeks, & a Schooner partly loaden with Salt, belonging to our town was Jan'y 4 driven out to Sea dragging her Anchors after, & not yet heard of nobody being aboard to

direct her Course, The Lord wean us from fading & perishing
Riches Amen. At our Dec'r Court Mr. J. Spark was wholly dis-
mist from being an Attorney for intemperance &c. Telix quem
faciunt aliend pericula cautum
Let him that thinks he stands take heed lest he fall
Be not high minded but fear —
And oh that we may all fear him who is able to keep us from
falling [into Sin or mischeif] & to present us faultless before the
presence of his glory with exceeding Joy; To whom be praise &
Glory now & forever Amen ———

---

*The Brethren in Colonial America: A Source Book on the Trans-
plantation and Development of the Church of the Brethren in the
Eighteenth Century, Donald F. Durnbaugh, ed.*
                    Elgin, Illinois, The Brethren Press, 1967, pp. 42–45

Pennsylvania, November 25, 1738

VERY ESTEEMED SIR AND FRIEND:

Although not all of those of us undersigned know you per-
sonally — in fact, only a very few do — we have yet been led
by various good reports of your kindness to take the liberty of
addressing to you this following communication to our countrymen who are filled with such an overwhelming desire to
migrate to this land and are still being stirred up to do so. We
also ask you kindly to publish this communication, as it is for
the benefit of the public, as early as possible, so that the poor
people are at least well informed, challenged, and brought to a
more mature consideration of their outward undertaking and
plans.

We, the undersigned, along with many of like mind, herewith write to you, our European and, especially German,
countrymen, who have been filled with such a strong desire
to migrate to this land. We send you first of all our friendly

greetings and ask you herewith to consider very seriously what kind of intention or spirit it is that moves you to such a general commotion and to undertake such an indescribably difficult move with your families. Is it really divine providence and will that motivates you? If it is, then this very hand of God would aid you in all situations, and would help bring you to your desired end and goal. (But alas!) is it not perhaps rather a long-lived and fearful secret desire to escape because of fear, and from waiting for events to come, and judgments, which really ought to cause repentance and betterment of heart? Or is it an imagined hope for an earthly paradise which may be attained? Or whether, as is well known and true, [is it] the exaggerated letters of praise and unauthenticated accounts by a few moneybag brethren [*Reichmanns Brüder*] and the generally greedy and selfish decoy birds [*Lock-Vögel*] and so-called Newlanders who are a special divine judgment and the real agitators in these troubled times, which were caused by the heavy pressure of the authorities through the very same divine verdict?

Whichever of these latter causes it might be, we are all compelled and feel obligated, for your own good, to give you a thorough account of the nature of this country, of the migration, sea voyage, and arrival of the German passengers in general and also, in particular, a conscientious and authenticated account of the indeed numerous but also miserable migrations of this year. Whether you believe it or not, time and experience of the historical truth will testify that we have not withheld such from you.

Fifty years ago the country of Pennsylvania, by an especially beneficial providence of God, was opened and offered to the foreigners and refugees persecuted here and there in Europe and in Old England who would gladly support themselves by their hands and diligence under divine protection and blessing. Our dear forefathers as the first inhabitants of this land consisted of Swedes, Englishmen, Germans, and Dutch. After breaking the ice and enduring many a difficulty, they lived a long time in considerable fear of God, righteousness, and genuine neighborly love as well as untiring industry, so that in some of their old people still living a rather exemplary pattern of their first love and unpartisan mutual friendship toward all nationalities, especially toward right-minded people, can still be seen.

However, since there were not many of them at that time, and the news spread, little by little many others arrived, of whom the majority acted against the very aim of the esteemed founder. They sought to gain much property and land and at the same time accumulated great wealth. Thus, along with other nationalities, many Germans who heard of this were enticed and persuaded and have migrated here and are still doing so every year because of ungodly purposes in order to become rich and grand. However, already several times — and it seems to be so again this year — the stars in their courses have crossed them through divine judgment, and hundreds, yes, even thousands, of them have been buried at sea without seeing the imagined promised land.

To be true, the country has until now had its generous blessings for hearts and stomachs, timber and water, bread and meat, flax and wool enough to satiation and shelter and beyond. Yet, it has become so crowded with people that, since it is very fruitful and for many years now large numbers of English, Irish, Scots, Germans, not to mention the slaves, have immigrated annually, it will see in perhaps twenty years hence more people than in the most populous countries over there.

Yet, on the other hand, there is less trade, commerce, and provisions than there, for in this country there is a shortage of money (even though it is only paper money which, however, has a certain fixed amount as high [as], yes, even higher than, over there) because of the great numbers of people who are already here. This is the reason for borrowing being so common here, among farmers and craftsmen, among great and small, so much so that hardly a place could be found in the old country, where the borrowing and frequent failure to repay is as common as here. It has been increasing continually, so that in the twelve, fifteen, to twenty years that we here can remember, it has become worse every year.

Also, because of the number of people who have immigrated and the increase in population, the good land has become so rare that it is to be considered good fortune when someone finds a good piece of land with all of the necessities provided, for which, accordingly, he must pay a high enough price even if it is far from Philadelphia, the only large city in the country. That which twenty or thirty years ago cost sixty or ninety guilders is now worth four hundred, six hundred, indeed, even one to two thousand guilders, namely for uncultivated and untilled land. There is, to be sure, still good and cheap land in Virginia and Maryland where many migrate, including old residents from here. However, the distance from this city is all the more difficult [to travel] when one has to travel two, three, or four weeks by horse and wagon in order to sell his crops and buy other necessities. Land here near the city is so expensive that a single acre costs sixty, one hundred to two hundred guilders, yes, even much more, without buildings, depending on its location.

The majority of those who are not long-time, wealthy, debt-free residents or very rich newcomers, must work strenuously and are hard put to earn a living, for there is neither baker nor butcher, salt nor spices, wine, nor brandy, physician nor barber, medicines nor schools to be found for miles around. Also, because of the lack of money they cannot very well live there, so that almost everything must be brought from and secured in the city under great difficulties. This is the reason why even wealthy people who are immigrating these days have regretted their move and wish themselves back over there once again. There are said to be many who would not hesitate to return again if it were not for the difficult journey. Some have already done this and are content with poorer circumstances than they once had. As was mentioned, land near the city being extremely expensive and wood and rent very high, it requires a real pouchful of money or a good income in order to rent for any length of time. So much for the country. . . .

HENRY GRAFF *in Amwell*
[*and 13 others*]

Documents Relative to the Colonial History of the State of New-York . . ., E. B. O'Callaghan, ed.
Albany, 1855, VI, pp. 197–198, 201–203

LIEUTENANT-GOVERNOR CLARKE TO THE LORDS OF TRADE.

New York June the 20, 1741.

MY LORDS

Before the Assembly rose I had the honor to receive a letter from his Grace the Duke of Newcastle signifying his Majesty's Commands to me to raise what recruits or new levies the General of the forces on the Expedition should write for, I recommended it to the Assembly to make provision before they rose for victualling and transporting them, lest if I raise them during their recess the service should be delayed, they on the contrary resolved to take it into consideration at their next meeting expecting that in the mean while I shall raise them and send them, drawing as Mr Thomas the Govr of Pensilvania did on the Commissioners of the Navy for the troops he raised last year, the truth is that seeing in the Philadelphia News Paper of the 14 of last month that Mr Thomas had drawn for the whole expence and that his bills are paid they believe that I might have done the same and saved them £2500 and are, I fear determined to be at no more expence tho they wont say so, however I will do all I can both to raise men and to bring to

pay the charge of victualling and transporting them; I
expect likewise to meet with great difficulties in raising
men at the time, for the confusion which the conspiracy
some white people and the Negroes entred into burn
this town and to destroy the inhabitants has begat a general opinion that no man ought to leave his habitation to
go out of the Province and the apprehension of a French
warr as this is a frontier Province will make every one,
who has any thing at stake industrious to discourage men
from inlisting themselves for this expedition lest a rup-
ture with France should soon happen, these are my apprehensions, however I will use my utmost application
to raise recruits when the General writes for them, for
as I did last year raise a greater proportion of Troops
than any of our Neighbouring Colonies, as will I believe
evidently appear by examining the lists of white people
in the Colonies, I shall be very sorry to fall short now.

Harvest drawing nigh the Country members were im-
patient to go home so that I was obliged to adjourn the
Assembly till the middle of September, after they had
passed two Bills, One to build the Secretaries Office, Bar-
racks in the Fort, a Battery in this Town and to fortify
Oswego; The other to obliged the people of this Town
to a military night Guard.

(The fatal fire that consumed the buildings in the fort
and a great part of my substance, for my loss is not less
than two thousands pounds, did not happen by accident
as I at first apprehended, but was kindled by design in the
execution of a horrid Conspiracy to burn it and the whole
town and to Massacre the people, as appears evidently
not only by the Confession of the Negro who set fire to it
in some part of the same gutter where the Plumber was
to work but also by the testimony of several witnesses,
how many Conspirators there we do not yet know every
day produces new discoveries and I apprehend that in
the town, if the truth were known, there are not many in-

nocent Negromen, and it is thought that some Negroes of the Country are accomplices and were to act their part there, and to this belief I am led by the villany committed in New Jersey sometime after the fort was burnt, for at a Village called New wark seven Barnes were burnt in one night, for which two Negroes were tried and executed; In this Town there have been already executed for this Conspiracy seventeen vizt Three Whites (Huson the contriver and main spring of the whole design, his wife and another white woman who lived in Huson's house, and had a bastard by one of the Negro Conspirators) and fourteen Negroes. Huson is hung in chains, for the rest that or may be executed, I desired the Judges to single out only a few of the most notorious for execution, and that I would pardon the rest, on condition that the pardon be void if they be found in the Province after a certain day, whereby their masters will transport them out of hand, I do myself the honor to send your Lordships the minutes taken at the tryal of Quack who burned the fort, and of another Negro who was tryed with him, and their confession at the stake, with some other examinations, whereby your Lordships will see their designs, it was ridiculous to suppose that they could keep possession of the Town, if they had destroyed the White people, yet the mischief they would have done in pursuit of their intention would never the less have been great.

My loss sits very heavy upon me, His Majesties bounty and goodness, I am sensible are vastly great, but yet I know not how to hope for relief, unless thro the protection of his Grace the Duke of Newcastle, upon your Lordships favourable recommendation which I beg leave to ask.

Whether or how far the hand of popery has been in this hellish conspiracy I cannot yet discover, but there is room to suspect it, by what two of the Negroes have confest, Viz^t that soon after they were spoke to, and had consented to be parties to it, they had some checks of conscience which they said, would not suffer them to burn houses and kill the White people; whereupon those who drew them into the conspiracy told them, there was no sin or wickedness in it, and that if they would go to Huson's house, they should find a man who would satisfy them but they say they would not nor did go; Margaret. Keny was supposed to be a papist, and it is suspected that Huson and his wife were brought over to it: there was in Town some time ago a man who is said to be a Romish Priest, who used to be at Huson's, but has disappeared ever since the discovery of the conspiracy and is not now to be found, upon this occasion I do myself the honor to send your Lordships a paragraph of General Oglethorps letter to me.

I do myself the honor to send your Lordships the naval officers accounts for the last year, and I have the pleasure to say that if your Lordships will be pleased to compare those of the last three years with those of three years before I had the Government, you will see that the trade and navigation of the Province is greatly increased. I am with the highest respect and honor

> *My Lords*
> *Your Lordships*
> *most humble and*
> *most obedient Servant*
> GEO: CLARKE

LIEUTENANT-GOVERNOR CLARKE TO THE LORDS OF TRADE.

New York August the 24, 1741.

MY LORDS,

A. In my letter of the 20 of June I did myself the honor to inform your Lordships of the Plot to destroy this Town and people, but whatever I then said or could say falls

short of what has since appeared; We then thought it was
projected only by Huson and the Negroes but it is now
apparent that the hand of Popery is in it, for a Romish
Priest having been tryed was upon full and clear evidence
convicted of having a deep share in it we have besides
several other white men in prison and most of them (it is
thought) I wish Papists, one of whom is a dancing master,
some of them Soldiers in the two companies posted in
this town, and the father and three brothers of that Huson who was hanged, Where by whom or in what shape
this plot was first projected is yet undiscovered that
which at present seems most probable is that Huson an
indigent fellow of vile character casting in his thoughts
how to mend his circumstances inticed some Negroes to
rob their masters and to bring the stolen to him on promise of reward when they were sold but seeing that by this
pilfering trade riches did not flow into him fast enough
and finding the Negroes fit instruments for any villany
he then fell upon the schemes of burning the fort and
town and murdering the people as the speediest way to
enrich himself and them, and to gain the freedom, for
that was the Negroes main inducement, how long this
Plot has been on foot is uncertain one of the Negroes
who laid hold on my proclamation owned he was sworn
by Huson last Christmas was three years, others two years
ago others more lately but when or by what means the
Priest and Huson became acquainted is but conjecture
most likely it was by the means of Margaret Kerry who
lived in Husons house and was executed with him for
she being a profest Papist might disclose it to the Priest,
be that as it will after he was acquainted with them the
design seemed to proceed with more vigour. The conspirators had hopes given them that the Spaniards would
come hither and join with them early in the Spring but
if they failed of coming then the business was to be done
by the Conspirators without them many of them were

christen'd by the Priest absolved of all their past sins and whatever they should do in the Plott many of them sworn by him (others by Huson to burn and destroy and to be secret, wherein they were but too punctual how weak soever the scheme may appear it was plausible and strong enough to engage and hold the Negroes and that was all that the Priest and Huson wanted for had the fort taken fire in the night as it was intended the town was then to have been fired in several places at once, in which confusion much rich Plunder might have been got and concealed and if they had it in view too, to serve the enemy they could not have done it more effectually for this town being laid in Ashes his Majesties forces in the West Indies might have suffered much for want of provisions and perhaps been unable to proceed upon any expedition or peice of service, from whence they might promise themselves great rewards, I doubt the business is pretty nigh at an end for since the Priest has been apprehended and some more white men named, great industry has been used through out the town to discredit the witnesses and prejudice the people against them and I am told it has had in a great measure its intended effect I am sorry for it for I do not think we are yet got near the bottom of it, when I doubt the principal conspirators lie concealed.

B. I have the honor to inform your Lordships that by the means of some people whom I sent last year to reside in the Senecas country (as usual) I obtained a deed for the lands at Tierrondequat from the Sachimes and I have sent orders to those people to go round the lands in Company with some of the Sachims and to mark the trees, that it may be known at all times hereafter how much they have given up to us.

C. General Oglethorp by his letter of the 12 of the last month acquaints me that the Creeks and Cherokees being by him informed of the treaty made last year at

Albany by me with the Six Nations are much pleased with it and propose to send deputies thither but as his Majesty has been pleased to appoint Commodore Clinton to be Governor of this Province who hopes to be here the later end of this or the beginning of the next month it must be left to him to do therein as he thinks proper. I am very glad that he will find the Province in great tranquility and in a flourishing condition able to support the Government in an honorable and ample manner and I hope he will bring them to do it, wherein nothing shall be wanting on my part.

D. My great losses in the fire at the fort, after a very expensive year in promoting the expedition &^{c} sit very heavy upon me; and I again beg leave to intreat your Lordships to recommend me to the Protection of his Grace the Duke of Newcastle hoping that thereby his noble and generous nature may be wrought upon to keep me by some means or other from sinking under the weight of my misfortunes, I am infinitely bound to his Grace for his protection hitherto which I shall acknowledge as long as I live with the highest thankfulness and to your Lordships I beg leave to return my most humble thanks for all your favours and goodness to me, beseeching you to assist me in this my time of need, to which I am reduced by this execrable Plott.

E. I do myself the honor to send your Lordships the two Acts past the last sitting of the Assembly Viz^t An Act for the morequal keeping military Watches in the City of New York and for other the purposes therein mentioned.

The reason for passing this Act appears in the preamble.

An Act for the better fortifying of this Colony and other the purposes therein mentioned. In this Act your Lordships may be pleased to see that I have got the Assembly to put this Town in a better posture of defence, to build the Secretaries office and a Barrack all of them necessary workes. I likewise prevailed with them to fortify Oswego, and to give an hundred pounds to be applyed in buying provisions for the relief of the Indians who were in great want, from the length and severity of the last winter, and I am perswaded, that this Act of Humanity will be remembered by them at all times with gratitude.

F. I have the honor to receive your Lordships letter of the 17th of April with the two Acts of Parliament.

G. I beg leave before I conclude to acquaint your Lordships that of the conspirators there have been executed Three Whites and twenty nine Negroes, pardoned one white Woman, vizt Husons daughter and pardoned and transported eighty Negroes besides eight Negroes not indicted but being accused and strongly suspected to be guilty their masters consented to transport them.

Ury whose tryal I sent your Lordships is sentenced to be hanged.

I repreived him for a few days upon his Petition for a short time to prepare himself but that being expired he is by rule of Court made since to be executed next Saturday. I humbly recommend myself to your Lordships protection and am with the highest respect and honor

My Lords
Your Lordships
most humble and
most obedient Servant
Geo: Clarke.

The Spread of
CHAPTER 2   Evangelical Pietism
in North America

George Whitefield represented not only a new movement of spiritual concern and rejuvenation, but also new techniques of communicating this concern to the populace. Whitefield was a magnificent and practiced public orator, who knew how to manipulate crowd reaction and excitement to his purposes. Unlike parish ministers, who lived with their flocks for years and instructed them in the ethical and moral values of Christianity — a tedious business — Whitefield itinerated and preached solely for conversions. Soon colonial clergymen, many of them frustrated in their own parishes, joined Whitefield on the revival "trail." The Awakening spread rapidly thereafter.

Almost without exception, Americans at first responded favorably to the message of Whitefield and his fellow pietists, but the concern of the evangelicals with visible and sudden evidences of God's grace (which they considered necessary for "conversion") soon produced occurrences which distressed many colonials, both laymen and clergy. From the beginning, most of Whitefield's fellow Anglican missionaries suspected his doctrine and orthodoxy, and soon Anglican opponents were joined by Presbyterian ministers (called "Old Sides") who objected to the embracing of Whitefield and revivalism by Gilbert Tennent and his friends. It was in New England, however, that the clergy was sharply divided between proponents and opponents of Whitefield and the Awakening. This clerical split exaggerated already unstable conditions in New England Puritanism (and other denominations as well) to produce a number of schisms and separations within individual congregations. In many cases the issues were not doctrinal in nature, but in Connecticut there developed a cadre of pro-revivalists who were more than mere supporters of the Awakening. These people had a very radical program of religious reformation which led them to reject the existing churches in their colony; many ultimately cast aside infant baptism. These radicals — the Separates or Separate Baptists — were not only disturbers of the status quo in church and state, but also hyperactive itinerant missionaries who transported their version of evangelical pietism to every corner of British North America, especially to the newly-settled regions.

Some distinction should probably be maintained between the great and general outburst of spiritual concern of the early 1740's — the Great Awakening proper — and the extension of evangelical pietism in America which continued throughout the eighteenth century and beyond. The pietists, especially the Baptists and later the Methodists, were particularly successful in the backcountry regions, where clergymen were in short supply, because they cared little about formal requirements such as education or ordination for their missionaries and were willing to take religion to the people in a manner popularly acceptable and comprehensible. Thus revivalism became a permanent condition of the expansion of American settlement.

The following selections from George Whitefield's journals (published first in 1741 soon after they were written and widely circulated) give Whitefield's own version of his intentions, techniques, and opposition.

GEORGE WHITEFIELD
George Whitefield's Journals.
London, The Banner of Truth Trust, 1960, pp. 400–401, 419–420, 457–463

CHARLESTON

Friday, March 14 [1740]: Arrived last night at Charleston, being called there to see my brother, who lately came from England, and had brought me a packet of letters from my dear friends. Blessed be God, His work goes on amongst them! Waited on the Commissary, with my brother and other companions; but met with a cool reception. After I had been there a little while, I told him I was informed he had some questions to propose to me, and that I had now come to give him all the satisfaction I could in answering them. Upon this, I immediately perceived passion to arise in his heart. "Yes, Sir," he said, "I have several questions to put to you. But," he added, "you have got above us," or something to that effect. Then he charged me with enthusiasm and pride, for speaking against the generality of the clergy, and desired I would make my charge good. I told him, I thought I had already; though as yet I had scarce begun with them. He then asked me wherein the clergy were so much to blame? I answered, they did not preach justification by faith alone; and upon talking with the Commissary, I found he was as ignorant as the rest. He then sneered me with telling me of my modesty, expressed in my letter to the Bishop of Gloucester; charged me with breaking the Canons and Ordination vow; and, notwithstanding I informed him I was ordained by Letters Dismissory from the Bishop of London, in a great rage, he told me, if I preached in any public church in that province, he would suspend me. I replied, I should regard that as much as I would a Pope's bull. "But, Sir," I said, "why should you be offended at my speaking against the generality of the clergy; for I always spoke well of you?" "I might as well be offended," added my brother, "at you saying, 'the generality of people were notorious sinners,' and come and accuse you of speaking evil of me, because I was one of the people." I further added, "You did not behave thus, when I was with you last." "No," he said, "but you did not speak against the clergy then." I then said to him, "If you will make an application to yourself, be pleased to let me ask you one question, 'Have you delivered your soul by exclaiming against the assemblies and balls here?'" "What," said he, "must you come to catechise me? No, I have not exclaimed against them; I think there is no harm in them." "Then," I replied, "I shall think it my duty to exclaim against you." "Then, Sir," he said in a very great rage, "Get you out of my house." I and my friends then took our leave, pitying the Commissary, who I really thought was more noble than to give such treatment. After this, we went to public prayers, dined at a friend's house, drank tea with the Independent minister, and preached at four in the afternoon, to a large auditory in his meeting-house.

Saturday, March 15. Breakfasted, sang a hymn, and had some religious conversation on board my brother's ship. Preached in the Baptist meeting-house; and was much pleased, when I heard afterwards, that from the same pulpit, a person not long ago had preached, who denied the doctrine of original sin, the Divinity and Righteousness of our Lord, and the operation of God's Blessed Spirit upon the soul. I was led to shew the utter inability of man to save himself, and absolute necessity of his dependence on the rich mercies and free grace of God in Christ Jesus for his restoration. Some, I observed, were put under concern; and most seemed willing to know whether those things were so. In the evening, I preached again in the Independent meeting-house to a more attentive auditory than ever; and had the pleasure, afterwards, of finding that a gentlewoman, whose whole family had been carried away for some time with Deistical principles, began now to be unhinged, and to see that there was no rest in such a scheme for a fallen creature to rely on. Lord Jesus, for Thy mercies' sake, reveal Thyself in her heart, and make her willing to know the faith as it is in Thee. Amen.

PHILADELPHIA

Thursday, May 8. Had what my body much wanted, a thorough night's repose. Was called up early in the morning, as I always am, to speak to poor souls under convictions. The first who came was an Indian trader, whom God was pleased to bring home by my preaching when here last. He is just come from the Indian nation, where he has been praying with and exhorting all he met who were willing to hear. He has hopes of some of the Indians; but his fellow-traders endeavoured to prejudice them against him. However, he proposes to visit them again in the autumn, and I humbly hope the Lord will open a door amongst the poor heathen. The conversion of one of their traders, I take to be one great step towards it. Lord, carry on the work begun. Fulfil Thy ancient promises, and let Thy Son have the heathen for His inheritance, and the utmost parts of the earth for His possession.

I conversed also with a poor negro woman, who has been visited in a very remarkable manner. God was pleased to convert her by my preaching last autumn; but being under dejections on Sunday morning, she prayed that salvation might come to her heart, and that the Lord would be pleased to manifest Himself to her soul that day. Whilst she was at meeting, hearing Mr. M——n, a Baptist preacher, the Word came with such power to her heart, that at last she was obliged to cry out; and a great concern fell upon many in the congregation. The minister stopped, and several persuaded her to hold her peace; but she could not help praising and blessing God. Many since this have called her mad, and said she was full of new wine; but the account she gave me was rational and solid, and, I believe in that hour the Lord Jesus took a great possession of her soul. Such cases, indeed, have not been very common; but when an extraordinary work is being carried on, God generally manifests Himself to some souls in this extraordinary manner. I doubt not, when the poor negroes are to be called, God will highly favour them, to wipe off their reproach, and shew that He is no respecter of persons, but that whosoever believeth in Him shall be saved.

Preached, at eleven, to six or seven thousand people, and cleared myself from some aspersions that had been cast upon my doctrine, as though it tended to Antinomianism. I believe God has much people in the city of Philadelphia. The congregations are very large and serious, and I have scarce preached this time amongst them without seeing a stirring amongst the dry bones. At five in the evening I preached again, but to a rather larger audience; and, after sermon, rode ten miles to a friend's house, that I might be in readiness to preach the next morning, according to appointment. How differently am I treated from my Master! He taught the people by day, and abode all night upon the Mount of Olives. He had not where to lay His head; but go where I will, I find people receiving me into their houses with great gladness. . . .

BOSTON

Friday, September 19. I was visited by several gentlemen and ministers, and went to the Governor's with Esquire Willard, the Secretary of the Province, a man fearing God, and with whom I have corresponded some time, though before unknown in person. The Governor received me with the utmost respect, and desired me to see him as often as I could. At eleven, I went to public worship at the Church of England, and afterwards went home with the Commissary, who had read prayers. He received me very courteously; and, it being a day whereon the clergy of the Established Church met, I had an opportunity of conversing with five of them together. I think, one of them began with me for calling "that Tennent and his brethren *faithful* ministers of Jesus Christ." I answered, "I believed they were." They then questioned me about "the validity of the Presbyterian ordination." I replied, "I believed it was valid."

They then urged against me a passage in my first *Journal*, where I said, "That a Baptist minister at Deal did not give a satisfactory answer concerning his mission." I answered, "Perhaps my sentiments were altered." "And is Mr. Wesley altered in his sentiments?" said one; "for he was very strenuous for the Church, and rigorous against all other forms of government when he was at Boston." I answered, "He was then a great bigot, but God has since enlarged his heart, and I believed he was now like-minded with me in this particular." I then urged, "That a catholic spirit was best, and that a Baptist minister had communicated lately with me at Savannah." "I suppose," said another, "you would do him as good a turn, and would communicate with him." I answered, "Yes," and urged "that it was best to preach the new birth, and the power of godliness, and not to insist so much on the form: for people would never be brought to one mind as to that; nor did Jesus Christ ever intend it." "Yes, but He did," said Dr. Cutler. "How do you prove it?" "Because Christ prayed, 'That all might be one, even as Thou Father and I are One.'" I replied, "That was spoken of the inward union of the souls of believers with Jesus Christ, and not of the outward Church." "That cannot be," said Dr. Cutler, "for how then could it be said, 'that the world might know that Thou hast sent Me?'" He then (taking it for granted that the Church of England was the only true apostolical Church) drew a parallel between the Jewish and our Church, urging how God required all things to be made according to the pattern given in the Mount. I answered, "That before the parallel could be just, it must be proved, that every thing enjoined in our Church was as much of a Divine institution as any rite or ceremony under the Jewish dispensation." I added further, "That I saw regenerate souls among the Baptists, among the Presbyterians, among the Independents, and among the Church folks, — all children of God, and yet all born again in a different way of worship: and who can tell which is the most evangelical?" "What, can you see regeneration with your eyes?" said the Commissary, or words to that effect.

Soon after, we began to talk of the Righteousness of Christ, and the Commissary said, "Christ was to make up for the defects of our righteousness." I asked him, "Whether conversion was not instantaneous?" He was unwilling to confess it, but he having just before baptised an infant at public worship, I asked him, "Whether he believed that very instant in which he sprinkled the child with water, the Holy Ghost fell upon the child?" He answered, "Yes." "Then," said I, "according to your own principles, regeneration is instantaneous, and since you will judge of the new birth by the fruits, pray watch that child, and see if it brings forth the fruits of the Spirit." I also said, "That if every child was really born again in baptism, then every baptised infant would be saved." "And so they are," said Dr. Cutler. "How do you prove that?" "Because the Rubric says, 'that all infants dying after baptism before they have committed actual sin, are undoubtedly saved.'" I asked, "What text of Scripture there was to prove it?" "Here," said he, (holding a Prayer Book in his hand) "the Church says so." We then just hinted at predestination. I said, "I subscribed to the seventeenth Article of the Church in its literal sense with all my heart." We then talked a little about falling away finally from grace. I said, "A true child of God, though he might fall foully, yet could never fall finally." "But," said he, the Article says, " 'Men may fall away from grace given.'" I answered, "But then observe what follows 'and by the grace of God they may rise again.'" Several other things of less consequence passed between us. Finding how inconsistent they were, I took my leave, resolving they should not have an opportunity of denying me the use of their pulpits. However, they treated me with more civility than any of our own clergymen have done for a long while. The Commissary very kindly urged me to dine with them; but, being pre-engaged, I went to my lodgings, and, in the afternoon, preached to about four thousand people in Dr. Colman's meeting-house; and afterwards exhorted and prayed with many who came to my lodgings, rejoicing at the prospect there was of bringing many souls in Boston to the saving knowledge of the

Lord Jesus Christ. Grant this, O Father, for Thy dear Son's sake! Amen.

Saturday, September 20. Was refreshed with several packets of letters sent to me from different parts of England and America, giving me an account of the success of the Gospel. Yet I was a little cast down to find some English friends had thrown aside the use of means, and others were disputing for *sinless perfection* and *universal redemption*. I know no such things asserted in the Gospel, if explained aright. Lord, do Thou cause even this to work for good, and give me grace to oppose such errors, without respect of persons, but with meekness, humility and love. Amen.

Preached in the morning to about six thousand hearers, in the Rev. Dr. Sewall's meeting-house; and afterwards, on the common, to about eight thousand; and again, at night, to a thronged company at my lodgings. I spent the remainder of the evening with a few friends, in preparing for the Sabbath. Oh that we may be always in the Spirit on the Lord's Day!

Sunday, September 21. Went in the morning, and heard Dr. Colman preach. Dined with his colleague, the Rev. Mr. Cooper. Preached in the afternoon, to a thronged auditory, at the Rev. Mr. Foxcroft's meeting-house. Immediately after, on the common, to about fifteen thousand; and again, at my lodgings, to a greater company than before. Some afterwards came up into my room; and though hoarse, I was enabled to speak, and could have spoken, I believe, till midnight. To see people ready to hear, makes me forget myself. Oh that it may be my sleep, and my meat and drink to do the will of my Heavenly Father! Oh that all who press to hear the Word, may take the Kingdom of God by force! Amen and Amen.

Monday, September 22. Preached this morning at the Rev. Mr. Webb's meeting-house, to six thousand hearers in the house, besides great numbers standing about the doors. Most wept for a considerable time. Sometime after, I received a letter, wherein were these words: —

"But what I must give the preference to was that gracious season at the New North, the Monday following, where there was more of the presence of God through the whole visitation, than ever I had known through the whole course of my life. Justly might it have been said of that place, 'it was no other than the House of God and the Gate of Heaven!' O how dreadful was the place, and yet how delightful! The Lord Jesus seemed to be visibly walking in that His golden candlestick, to try some of the many thousands who were prepared for so holy an inquisition! I am sure I know none who could not but be humble at the thoughts of it. And who, indeed, could help crying out, 'Woe is me, for I am undone, because I am a man of unclean lips for mine eyes have seen the King, the Lord of Hosts.' The Spirit of God, indeed, seemed to be moving upon the face of the waters at that time, and who knows, but that to a great many souls, God was pleased to say, 'Let there be light, and there was light.' "

In the afternoon I went to preach at the Rev. Mr. Checkley's meeting-house; but God was pleased to humble us by a very awful providence. The meeting-house being filled, though there was no real danger, on a sudden all the people were in an uproar, and so unaccountably surprised, that some threw themselves out of the windows, others threw themselves out of the gallery, and others trampled upon one another; so that five were actually killed, and others dangerously wounded. I happened to come in the midst of the uproar, and saw two or three lying on the ground in a pitiable condition. God was pleased to give me presence of mind; so that I gave notice I would immediately preach upon the common. The weather was wet, but many thousands followed in the field, to whom I preached from these words, "Go out into the highways and hedges, and compel them to come in." I endeavoured, as God enabled me, to improve what had befallen us. Lord, Thy judgments are like the great deep. Thy footsteps are not known. Just and Holy art Thou, O King of saints!

In the evening, I was weak in body, so that I could not say much at the house where I supped; but God, by His Blessed Spirit, greatly refreshed and comforted my soul. I drank of God's pleasure as out of a river. Oh that all were made partakers of this living water: they would never thirst after the sensual pleasures of this wicked world.

Tuesday, September 23. Went this morning, with Dr. Colman and the Secretary to Roxbury, three miles from Boston, to see the Rev. Mr. Walter, a good old Puritan. He and his predecessor, the Rev. Mr. Eliot, commonly called the "Apostle of the Indians," now with God, have been pastors of that congregation a hundred and six years. I had but little conversation with him, my stay being very short.

At eleven we returned, and I preached in the Rev. Mr. Gee's meeting-house, but not to a very crowded auditory, because the people were in doubt where I would preach. Dined at the Secretary's; preached in the afternoon to a thronged congregation, and exhorted and prayed at my own lodgings. Lord, let Thy Presence always follow me, or otherwise I shall be but as a sounding brass or a tinkling cymbal.

Wednesday, September 24. Went this morning to see and preach at Cambridge, the chief college for training the sons of the prophets in New England. It has one president, four tutors, and about a hundred students. The college is scarce as big as one of our least colleges at Oxford; and, as far as I could gather from some who knew the state of it, not far superior to our Universities in piety. Discipline is at a low ebb. Bad books are become fashionable among the tutors and students. Tillotson and Clark are read, instead of Shepard, Stoddard, and such-like evangelical writers; and, therefore, I chose to preach from these words, — "We are not as many, who corrupt the Word of God." A great number of neighbouring ministers attended. God gave me great boldness and freedom of speech. The President of the college and minister of the parish treated me very civilly. In the afternoon, I preached again, in the court, when,

I believe, there were about seven thousand hearers. The Holy Spirit melted many hearts. A minister soon after wrote me word, "that one of his daughters was savingly wrought upon at that time." Lord, add daily to the Church, such as shall be saved! Paid my respects to the Lieutenant-Governor, who lives at Cambridge; and returned in the evening to Boston, and prayed with and exhorted many people who were waiting round the door for a spiritual morsel. I believe our Lord did not send them empty away. O Blessed Jesus, feed them with that Bread of Life Which cometh down from Heaven.

Thursday, September 25. Preached the weekly lecture at Mr. Foxcroft's meeting-house; but was oppressed with a sense of ingratitude to my Saviour, that Satan tempted me to hold my tongue, and not invite poor sinners to Jesus Christ, because I was so great a sinner myself. But God enabled me to withstand the temptation; and, since Jesus Christ had shewn such mercy to, and had not withdrawn His Holy Spirit from me, the chief of sinners, I was enabled more feelingly to talk of His love. I afterwards found that one stranger in particular, was in all probability convinced by that morning's sermon. After public worship, I went, at his Excellency's invitation, and dined with him. Most of the ministers of the town were invited with me. Before dinner, the Governor sent for me into his chamber. He wept, wished me good luck in the Name of the Lord, and recommended himself, ministers, and people to my prayers. Immediately after dinner, I prayed for them all; and then went in his carriage to the end of the town, crossed the ferry, and preached at Charleston, lying on the north side of Boston. The meeting-house was very capacious, and quite filled. A gracious melting was discernible through the whole congregation.

In the evening, I exhorted and prayed as usual, at my lodgings; and I found a great alteration in my hearers. They now began to melt and weep under the Word. Oh, that the Lord may beat them down with the hammer of His Word, till the heart of stone be entirely taken away! Amen, Lord Jesus.

ROXBURY

Friday, September 26. Preached in the morning at Roxbury to many thousands of people, from a little ascent. . . .

Blessed be God! for what He has done in Boston. I hope a glorious work is now begun, and that the Lord will stir up some faithful labourers to carry it on.

Boston is a large, populous place, and very wealthy. It has the form of religion kept up, but has lost much of its power. I have not heard of any remarkable stir for many years. Ministers and people are obliged to confess, that the love of many is waxed cold. Both seem to be too much conformed to the world. There is much of the pride of life to be seen in their assemblies. Jewels, patches, and gay apparel are commonly worn by the female sex. The little infants who were brought to baptism, were wrapped up in such fine things, and so much pains taken to dress them, that one would think they were brought thither to be initiated into, rather than to renounce, the pomps and vanities of this wicked world. There are nine meeting-houses of the Congregational persuasion, one Baptist, one French, and one belonging to the Scots-Irish. There are two monthly, and one weekly lectures; and those, too, but poorly attended. I mentioned it in my sermons, and I trust God will stir up the people to tread more frequently the courts of His house. One thing Boston is very remarkable for, viz., the external observance of the Sabbath. Men in civil offices have a regard for religion. The Governor encourages them; and the ministers and magistrates seem to be more united than in any other place where I have been. Both were exceedingly civil during my stay. I never saw so little scoffing, and never had so little opposition. Still, I fear, many rest in a head-knowledge, are close Pharisees, and have only a name to live. It must needs be so, when the power of godliness is dwindled away, where the form only of religion is become fashionable amongst people. However, there are "a few names left in Sardis, which have not defiled their garments." Many letters came to me from pious people, in which they complained of the degeneracy of the times, and hoped that God was about to revive His work in their midst. Even so, Lord Jesus, Amen and Amen. Yet Boston people are dear to my soul. They were greatly affected by the Word, followed night and day, and were very liberal to my dear orphans. I promised, God willing, to visit them again when it shall please Him to bring me again from my native country. . . .

The impact which Whitefield made in colonial America can be understood only by examining contemporary reactions. In the following passages, the rational and urbane Benjamin Franklin offers his views of the evangelist, while a semi-literate Connecticut farmer, Nathan Cole, describes his experiences at a Whitefield revival meeting.

The Autobiography of Benjamin Franklin, L. W. Labaree, et al., eds.
New Haven, Yale University Press, 1964, 176–180

Mr. Whitfield, in leaving us, went preaching all the Way thro' the Colonies to Georgia. The Settlement of that Province had lately been begun; but instead of being made with hardy industrious Husbandmen accustomed to Labour, the only People fit for such an Enterprise, it was with Families of broken Shopkeepers and other insolvent Debtors, many of indolent and idle habits, taken out of the Gaols, who being set down in the Woods, unqualified for clearing Land, and unable to endure the Hardships of a new Settlement, perished in Numbers, leaving many helpless Children unprovided for. The Sight of their miserable Situation inspired the benevolent Heart of Mr. Whitefield with the Idea of building an Orphan House there, in which they might be supported and educated. Returning northward he preach'd up this Charity, and made large Collections; for his Eloquence had a wonderful Power over the Hearts and Purses of his Hearers, of which I myself was an Instance. I did not disapprove of the Design, but as Georgia was then destitute of Materials and Workmen, and it was propos'd to send them from Philadelphia at a great Expence, I thought it would have been better to have built the House here and brought the Children to it. This I advis'd, but he was resolute in his first Project, and rejected my Counsel, and I thereupon refus'd to contribute. I happened soon after to attend one of his Sermons, in the Course of which I perceived he intended to finish with a Collection, and I silently resolved he should get nothing from me. I had in my Pocket a Handful of Copper Money, three or four Silver Dollars, and five Pistoles in Gold. As he proceeded I began to soften, and concluded to give the Coppers. Another Stroke of his Oratory made me asham'd of that, and determin'd me to give the Silver; and he finish'd so admirably, that I empty'd my Pocket wholly into the Collector's Dish, Gold and all. At this Sermon there was also one of our Club, who being of my Sentiments respecting the Building in Georgia, and suspecting a Collection might be intended, had by Precaution emptied his Pockets before he came from home; towards the Conclusion of the Discourse however, he felt a strong Desire to give, and apply'd to a Neighbour who stood near him to borrow some Money for the Purpose. The Application was unfortunately to perhaps the only Man in the Company who had the firmness not to be affected by the Preacher. His Answer was, *At any other time, Friend Hopkinson, I would lend to thee freely; but not now; for thee seems to be out of thy right Senses.*

Some of Mr. Whitfield's Enemies effected to suppose that he would apply these Collections to his own private Emolument; but I, who was intimately acquainted with him, (being employ'd in printing his Sermons and Journals, &c.) never had the least Suspicion of his Integrity, but am to this day decidedly of Opinion that he was in all his Conduct, a perfectly *honest Man.* And methinks my Testimony in his Favour ought to have the more Weight, as we had no religious Connection. He us'd indeed sometimes to pray for my Conversion, but never had the Satisfaction of believing that his Prayers were heard. Ours was a mere civil Friendship, sincere on both Sides, and lasted to his Death.

The following Instance will show something of the Terms on which we stood. Upon one of his Arrivals from England at Boston, he wrote to me that he should come soon to Philadelphia, but knew not where he could lodge when there, as he understood his old kind Host Mr. Benezet was remov'd to Germantown. My Answer was; You know my House, if you can make shift with its scanty Accommodations you will be most heartily welcome. He reply'd, that if I made that kind Offer for Christ's sake, I should not miss of a Reward. And I return'd, *Don't let me be mistaken; it was not for Christ's sake, but for your sake.* One of our common Acquaintance jocosely remark'd, that knowing it to be the Custom of the Saints, when they receiv'd any favour, to shift the Burthen of the Obligation from off their own Shoulders, and place it in Heaven, I had contriv'd to fix it on Earth.

The last time I saw Mr. Whitefield was in London, when he consulted me about his Orphan House Concern, and his Purpose of appropriating it to the Establishment of a College.

He had a loud and clear Voice, and articulated his Words and Sentences so perfectly that he might be heard and understood at a great Distance, especially as his Auditories, however numerous, observ'd the most exact Silence. He preach'd one Evening from the Top of the Court House Steps, which are in the Middle of Market Street, and on the West Side of Second Street which crosses it at right angles. Both Streets were fill'd with his Hearers to a considerable Distance. Being among the hindmost in Market Street, I had the Curiosity to learn how far he could be heard, by retiring backwards down the Street towards the River, and I found his Voice distinct till I came near Front-Street, when some Noise in that Street, obscur'd it. Imagining then a Semi-Circle, of which my Distance should be the Radius, and that it were fill'd with Auditors, to each of whom I allow'd two square feet, I computed that he might well

be heard by more than Thirty-Thousand. This reconcil'd me
to the Newspaper Accounts of his having preach'd to 25000
People in the Fields, and to the antient Histories of Generals
haranguing whole Armies, of which I had sometimes doubted.

By hearing him often I came to distinguish easily between
Sermons newly compos'd, and those which he had often
preach'd in the Course of his Travels. His Delivery of the latter
was so improv'd by frequent Repetitions, that every Accent,
every Emphasis, every Modulation of Voice, was so perfectly
well turn'd and well plac'd, that without being interested in the
Subject, one could not help being pleas'd with the Discourse, a
Pleasure of much the same kind with that receiv'd from an excellent Piece of Musick. This is an Advantage itinerant Preachers have over those who are stationary: as the latter cannot
well improve their Delivery of a Sermon by so many Re-
hearsals.

His Writing and Printing from time to time gave great Advantage to his Enemies. Unguarded Expressions and even erro-
neous Opinions del[ivere]d in Preaching might have been afterwards explain'd, or qualify'd by supposing others that might
have accompany'd them; or they might have been deny'd; But
litera scripta manet. Critics attack'd his Writings violently, and
with so much Appearance of Reason as to diminish the Number of his Votaries, and prevent their Encrease. So that I am
of Opinion, if he had never written any thing he would have
left behind him a much more numerous and important Sect.
And his Reputation might in that case have been still growing,
even after his Death; as there being nothing of his Writing on
which to found a censure; and give him a lower Character, his
Proselites would be left at liberty to feign for him as great a
Variety of Excellencies, as their enthusiastic Admiration might
wish him to have possessed.

G. L. WALKER
Some Aspects of the Religious Life of New England.
New York, 1897, pp. 89–92

[*October 23, 1740*]

Now it pleased god to send mr. whitfeld into this land &
my hearing of his preaching at philadelphia like one of the old
aposels, & many thousands floocking after him to hear yᵉ
gospel and great numbers were converted to Christ, i felt the
spirit of god drawing me by conviction i longed to see & hear
him & wished he would come this way and i soon heard he was
come to new york & yᵉ jases [Jerseys] & great multitudes flock-
ing after him under great concern for their Soule & many converted wich brought on my concern more & more hoping soon
to see him but next i herd he was on long iland & next at
boston & next at northampton & then one morning all on a
Suding about 8 or 9 o Clock there came a messenger & said
mr. whitfeld preached at hartford & weathersfield yesterday &
is to preach at middeltown this morning at 10 o clock i was in
my field at work i dropt my tool that i had in my hand & run
home & run throu my house & bad my wife get ready quick to
goo and hear mr. whitfield preach at middeltown & run to my
pasture for my hors with all my might fearing i should be too
late to hear him i brought my hors home & soon mounted &
took my wife up & went forward as fast as i thought yᵉ hors
could bear, & when my hors began to be out of breath i would
get down & put my wife on yᵉ Saddel & bid her ride as fast as
she could & not Stop or Slak for me except i bad her & so i
would run untill i was almost out of breth & then mount my
hors again & so i did severel times to favour my hors we improved every moment to get along as if we was fleeing for our
lives all this while fearing we should be too late to hear yᵉ Sar-
mon for we had twelve miles to ride dubble in littel more then
an hour & we went round by the upper housen parish & when
we came within about half a mile of yᵉ road that comes down

from hartford weathersfield & stepney to middeltown on high
land i saw before me a Cloud or fog rising i first thought off
from yᵉ great river but as i came nearer yᵉ road i heard a noise
something like a low rumbling thunder & i presently found it
was yᵉ rumbling of horses feet coming down yᵉ road & this
Cloud was a Cloud of dust made by yᵉ running of horses feet
it arose some rods into yᵉ air over the tops of yᵉ hills & trees &
when i came within about twenty rods of yᵉ road i could see
men & horses Sliping along in yᵉ Cloud like shadows & when i
came nearer it was like a stedy streem of horses & their riders
scarcely a horse more then his length behind another all of a
lather and some with swet ther breath rooling out of their
noistrels in yᵉ cloud of dust every jump every hors semed to
go with all his might to carry his rider to hear yᵉ news from
heaven for yᵉ saving of their Souls it made me trembel to see yᵉ
Sight how yᵉ world was in a strugle i found a vacance between
two horses to Slip in my hors & my wife said law our cloaths
will be all spoiled see how they look for they was so covered
with dust that thay looked allmost all of a coler coats & hats &
shirts & horses We went down in yᵉ Streem i herd no man speak
a word all yᵉ way three mile but evry one presing forward
in great hast & when we gat down to yᵉ old meating house thare
was a great multitude it was said to be 3 or 4000 of people asem-
bled together we gat of from our horses & shook off yᵉ dust
and yᵉ ministers was then coming to the meating house i turned
and looked toward yᵉ great river & saw the fery boats running
swift forward & backward bringing over loads of people yᵉ
ores roed nimble & quick every thing men horses & boats all
seamed to be struglin for life yᵉ land & yᵉ banks over yᵉ river
lookt black with people & horses all along yᵉ 12 miles i see no
man at work in his field but all seamed to be gone — when i see
mr. whitfield came up upon yᵉ Scaffil he looked almost an-
gellical a young slim slender youth before some thousands of
people & with a bold undainted countenance & my hearing
how god was with him every where as he came along it solum-
nized my mind & put me in a trembling fear before he began

to preach for he looked as if he was Cloathed with authority from ye great god, & a sweet sollome Solemnity sat upon his brow & my hearing him preach gave me a heart wound by gods blessing my old foundation was broken up & i saw that my righteousness would not save me then i was convinced of ye doctrine of Election & went right to quareling with god about it because all that i could do would not save me & he had decreed from Eternity who should be saved & who not i began to think i was not Elected & that god made some for heaven & me for hell & i thought god was not Just in so doing i thought i did not stand on even Ground with others if as i thought i was made to be damned my heart then rose against god exceedigly for his making me for hell now this distress lasted almost two years.

One of George Whitefield's earliest itinerant successors was the Voluntown, Connecticut, minister, Eleazer Wheelock (later the founder of Dartmouth College), whose preaching tour in 1741 is detailed in the following extract from his diary.

Historical Magazine, V, 1869, 237–240

[*Diary of Rev. Eleazer Wheelock, D.D., During his Visit to Boston, October 19, until November 16, 1741.*]

Oct. 19, 1741. I left my family under some difficulties, by reason of Betty's sickness and John's weakness, and was disappointed in my purpose to visit dear Mr. Kirtland, by reason that the flood had carried away the bridges; and with much difficulty arrived about 6 o'clock at Capt Johnson's, where we are courteously received. O that God would give me courage, zeal and skill to deal faithfully with my friends. God grant thy presence with me and my dear companion, in every place where we shall come.

Oct. 20. Preached at 10 with some inlargements, Present: Revs. Messrs. Coit, Kirtland, Dorrance, Barber, Avery, Wood, &c. The Assembly large and considerably affected. Dined at Bro. Woodworth's.

Preached in the afternoon at Plainfield to a full assembly, A number cry'd out. Held a conference at night — Young Christians dont rise, as in some places — One Converted — O when shall I learn to live always upon God, and be thankful for all the least inlargement and assistance?

21. Had little sleep; arose before day. Rode with Mr. Coit and my friends to Voluntown — went to meeting at 10, heard Mr. Gid: Mills preach well. I preached after him. There is a great work in this town, but more of the footsteps of Satan than in any place I have yet been in. The zeal of some too furious — they tell of many visions, revelations, and many Strong impressions upon their imagination. They have had much of God in many of their meetings, and his great power has been much seen, and many hopefully converted. Satan is using many artful wiles to put a stop to the word of God in this place. Went to the Conference at night, but was very low and flat in my Spirits for want of sleep. However, I mentioned to them some of those devices of Satan which I apprehended them in danger of, and heard the accounts of a number of new converts; prayed, sung, &c.

22. Rose this morning refreshed. A pleasant day. Found my soul stretching after God. Good Lord, let me not go alone. Dear Jesus, help thou me. The Lord has this day, in some measure, fulfilled my early desires. Preached twice with inlargement by Mr. Smith's barn to great assemblies. Many cried out, many stood trembling. The whole assembly very Solemn and much affected. 4 or 5 converted; one woman who came from Kingston against a great deal of opposition on purpose to hear me, came out clear, and went away rejoicing in God, longing to have her husband and others taste and see with her. Heard Mr. Mills preach in the evening from *John, iii. 5.* A very good Sermon it was. I think he is a very dear Brother.

23. Woke this morning about 3. Something indisposed. Dear Lord, I commit my body, my soul, my life, health, and all to thee; use me as thou wilt, only let me glorify thee, and seek that as my last end. Left Voluntown about 9, accompanied by a great number of wounded and comforted. I never heard so many imaginations as young Christians tell of here in my life, Some tell of a long course and series of them. . . . Came to Mr. Cooper's of Situate. Preached to a considerable assembly, but much spent. I am always thronged with company and han't time to talk with the 10th part of those who desire it. Dined and rode with a great number of Voluntown people to Capt Angill's; Preached there. . . . Rode with Lieut. Dorrance to Elder Fish's in hope to find him a Servant of Christ; but found him a bigoted ignorant Baptist, who seemed to know nothing as he ought to know &c. . . . Left him, and came about 8 to Mr. Henry's, about 4 miles from Providence. Received with love and respect. Found some good Christians, but myself much spent. O that I might be kept humble.

24. Rose early. Prayed and Sang. Discoursed with some wounded; afterwards exhorted a company who came in. Sang an Hymn, prayed, and rode with a great number of Voluntown people and others to Providence. About 2 miles from Providence met Mr. Knight and another man, who came out to meet us. His first salutation was — "God bless you, my dear Brother;" Went to his house; was treated with much friendship and respect by him and his family. Dined, Wrote, Prayed, Sang, spent the evening in Christian conversation; Revd Cotton came; invited me to preach; felt freedom and Sweetness in my Soul.

25. Rode with Mr. Knight into town in his Calashe. Preached 3 Sermons. *II Cor. xiii., 5, Mark i. 2, Luke, x. ult.* O the dreadful ignorance and wickedness of these parts. O what a burthen dear Mr. Cotton has daily to bear. Found Mr. Searing at Rode Island here.

26. Rode with Mr. Cotton back 7 miles to Mr. Bennit's. Preached at 1 o'clock to a numerous and affected Assembly.

One converted. Dined at Mr. Henry's. Returned with a great number to Providence. Preached to a full Assembly. Many Scoffers present. One man hired for 20 s. to come into the meeting house and fall down, which he did, and made great disturbance. Ordered all who had a real concern for the Salvation of their Souls to follow me to Mr. Cotton's in order to have a conference with them. A considerable number came. Many of them belonged to other places, who seemed considerably moved, and Christians enlivened. Exhorted, Sang, and prayed, and dismissed them.

27. Went with Mr. Cotton and Madam over the ferry to Rehoboth, upon Mr. Greenwood's invitation. Preached at 1. Rode in Mr. Cotton's calash with Madam, Mr. Cotton and my friends in company to Swansey. Came about 8 to John Finney's. Preached there, &c.

28. Br. Finney and his Br. John went to Dn. Kingsley's for liberty to preach in the Baptist meeting house, but he refused it. But Dn. —— sent for the Key and unlocked the doors. I went in and preached at 1, and again in the evening. O poor bigoted, ignorant, and prejudiced People. I went after meeting to Capt. Wm. Turner's, a Seperate Baptist. Was exceedingly pleas'd with his wife, a true and shining Christian, and a woman of great knowledge and prudence; her family exceedingly well governed by her. Stayed with them, and discoursed about their spiritual concerns, etc. I think that the principles of the Separate Baptists are the most uncharitable, unscriptural, and unreasonable that I have yet met with.

29. Came with Mr. Cotton, Madam and many more to Attleboro. Very courteously received by Mr. Wells. Heard Mr. Turner of Rehoboth, who seemed the day before to discourse very ignorantly about conversion; but my esteem of him is now raised by what I heard. Preached after him. A great deal of affection and sobbing, thro' the whole assembly. Had great inlargement. Exhorted in the evening at Mr. Wells.

30. Slept well last night. Had a great sense of my own badness and unworthiness, and what a cursed heart I have. O Lord,

let me see and know more of it. Rode with Mr. Wells and many others to Norton. Kindly received by Mr. Avery. Preached to a full assembly. Much affection and sobbing through the whole assembly. Rode after lecture to Taunton. Lodged at Madam Danford's; who lives with her daughter Hodge. Preached at 10. A great outcry in the Assembly. Many greatly wounded. Dined at Mr. Danford's, son to the former minister. Rode to Rainham with Mr. Wales and Br. Byram, who came to me at Norton. Conversed with my friends, . . . and wrote my Journal. O that I may be kept low in my own eyes.

Nov. 1. Rose this morning, was much pleas'd with the conversation of Mr. Wales and Madam. Preached in the forenoon to a full assembly. One cried out: many affected. Advised those who belonged to the assembly not to follow me to Taunton, but stay and hear their own Preacher. Went with Mr. Byram to Taunton. Preached there, *Job, xxvii. 8,* One or two cried out. Appointed another meeting in the evening. *Hos. xiii. 13.* I believed 30 cried out: almost all the negroes in the town wounded, 3 or 4 converted. A great work in the town. Dear Br. Crocker, a true Servant of Jesus Christ, preaches here upon probation. Colonel Leonard's negro in such distress that it took 3 men to hold him. I was forced to break off my Sermon before I had done, the outcry was so great. Continued the meeting till 10 or 11 o'clock. Went with Br. Crocker to his lodgings, Judge Williams's. Was kindly received.

2. Rode with Mr. Crocker to the tavern to see Capt. L——'s negro, Found him under a very clear and genuine conviction. Dear Br. Rogers came to me here. Rode with me to Mr. Weeks, and he joined us with a great number to Bridgewater. Preached to a full assembly in Mr. Shaw's meeting-house. Present, the Revd Messrs. Jno. Wales, Jon^a Patten, Mr. Cotton, Daniel Perkins, Jno. Shaw, Jno. Porter. Lodged with Mr. Parker, at Mrs. Shaws.

3. Rode with a great number to Mr. Perkins' meeting. Very full assembly. After Sermon the Lecture was appointed at Mr.

Auger's, but so many wounded that I could not leave them, and therefore preached again to a full assembly, *Ezek. xxii. 14.* A great outcry. 4 or 5 converted. Lodged with Dr. Wm. Rogers at Mr. Perkins'.

4. Rode to Mr. Porter's. A great multitude. Preached upon a Stage, (*Hos. xiii, 13.*) One converted in Serm. After dinner rode with Mr. Belcher and a great multitude to Easton. Br. Rogers preached. A very great outcry in the assembly. I preached after him, (*Acts, vii. 51.*) 4 or 5 converted. Lodged at Mr. Belcher's.

5. Came to Mr. Niles' of Braintery, [Braintree]. Preached with great freedom, (*II. Cor. xiii. 5.*) Present, Messrs. Eells and Handcock. Mr. Woster came in the evening.

6. Set out for Boston. Met my dear Mr. Prince, and Mr. Bromfield about 8 miles from Boston. Came in to Mr. Bromfield's. Received in a most kind and Christian manner by him, Madam and his family, a dear Christian family, full of Kindness, love and goodness. . . . His eldest son is now in his last year at Cambridge College. I believe a real converted person. Messrs. Price and Bromfield accompanied me back to Boston. Soon after I got into Mr. Bromfield's, came the Honorable Jos. Willard, Secret'y, Rev. Mr. Webb and Mr. Cooper, and Maj^r Sewall to bid me welcome to Boston. At 6 o'clock rode with Mr. Bromfield in his shays to the North End of the town and preached for Mr. Webb to a great Assembly, (*II. Cor. xiii. 5.*) After Sermon returned to dear Mr. Webbs, where I was pleased with the conversation of dear Mr. Gee. Returned with Mr. Bromfield.

7. Slept comfortably. Rose and prayed with Mr. Rogers. At 10, rode with Mr. Bromfield to Mr. Webb's. Preached (*Hos. xiii. 13,*) to a full assembly. Returned and was invited by Dr. Coleman and Mr. Cooper to preach for Dr. Coleman, in the forenoon the next day, being Sabbath, and by Mr. Prince and Dr. Sewall in the afternoon. Preached to the Workhouse, (*Ezek. xxii. 14.*)

8. Went to Dr. Coleman's meeting. Preached with considerable freedom, (*Job. xxvii. 8*). Dined with the Dr. Went with Br. Rogers to Mr. Prince's. Preached (*Mar. xxi. 16,*) to a full assembly. After meeting, was followed by a great throng of children, who importunately desired me to give them a word of exhortation in a private house, which I consented to, though I was designed to go and hear Mr. Prince, who, being by, desired that I would have it publickly, which I consented to. After 6 we met again. Preached (*Mat. vi. 33,*) to a very full assembly. Rode with Mr. Bromfield, in a close shays; followed to his house after me a great many children, to receive a word of exhortation at the gate, which I could not stand long to do, being very wet with sweat.

9. Visited this morning by a great number of persons under soul-trouble. Refused to preach because I designed [*going*] out of town. Discoursed with Mr. Bromfield's dear children. Took my leave, by prayer recommending them, and one another to the Lord. Just as I was going, came Mr. Webb, and told me the people were meeting together, to hear another Sermon, and said if I would not stay without they would hold me. At 4 P.M. I consented to preach again. A scholar from Cambridge being present, who came to get me to go to Cambridge, and by a little after 6, a great part of the scholars had got to Boston. Preached to a very thronged assembly, many more than could get into the house, (*Psa. xxxiv. 8,*) with very great freedom and inlargement. I [*consider*] the church of God were very much refreshed. They told me afterwards they believed that Mather Byles never was so lashed in his life. This morning Mr. Cooper came to me in the name of the Hon. Jacob Wendel, Esq., and earnestly desired a copy of my Sermon preached in the forenoon, Lord's day, for the press. O that God would make and keep me humble. Appointed to preach to-morrow for Mr. Balch of Dedham, at his desire.

10. Madam Bromfield gave me this morning a shirt and pair of gold buttons, two cambrick handkerchiefs, a pound of tea and part of a loaf of sugar, and he a preaching Bible in 2 vols. same that Dr. Hinchman, of whom he bought them, gave 11 s. [*for*] Came out of town with Mr. Dyre and another Gentleman. Met Mr. Cotton of Providence about 8 miles from Boston, who came at the desire and by the vote of his church to get me to come back that way, and informed me of some very good beginnings, and very hopeful appearances among his people and the people of other persuasions there, and was very importunate with me to go with him, but I tho't it my duty to go directly home, encouraging him that I would come or send to him before long. He accompanied me to Mr. Balch's. Preached (*Mark xvi. 16*). Went to Medfield.

11. Preached at 3 P.M. (*Mark, i. 2, 3,*) with some freedom. Went in the evening to see Mr. Baxter.

12. Being Thanksgiving, preached (*Ps. xxxiv. 8,*) and in the evening at Medway for Mr. Buck[*in*]ham. He seemed displeased that I told his people that Christians generally knew the time of their conversion. Returned to Uncle Adams's. Gave a word of exhortation, sang and prayed with a number of young people there.

13. Went with Uncles Wheelock, Adams, Aunt Wheelock, Elisha Adams and many more to Bellingham. Preached to a very large assembly in the woods, (*Mar. xvi. 16.*) Many appeared affected. Present, Messrs. Dor, Messenger and dear Mr. Havens. Went with Mr. Dor and dined at Mr. Obad. Wheelocks. Received and treated with much respect by him and family, and his brother Benjamin. Much importuned to preach at Mendom, [*Mendon*] but came to Uxbridge. Lodged at Woods, the tavern. Importuned to preach the next day, but tho't best to pursue my journey.

14. Came to Thompson. Preached three Sermons for Mr. Cabbot; one to the young people at night. Many affected.

16. Came to the Consociation at Windham, and after it, home about 1 o'clock. What shall I render to the Lord for all his benefits?

Emphasis on emotional "conversion experiences" of crisis proportion naturally produced some extravagances and excesses of behavior. Perhaps the most famous example of excess was provided by the activities of the Reverend James Davenport of New York. The scene of most of Davenport's extremities was New London, Connecticut. The following selections offer several views of Davenport in New London and elsewhere. Judge Joshua Hempstead offers a contemporary eyewitness account and reaction; the county court records present the formal "offenses" gossiped about in 1744 by Dr. Alexander Hamilton. Finally, Davenport's own "confession" offers perhaps the fullest picture of the magnitude of his "offenses" as perceived by his peers.

JOSHUA HEMPSTEAD

Diary of Joshua Hempstead of New London Connecticut Covering a Period of Forty-Seven Years from September, 1711, to November, 1758.

New London, *Collections of the New London County Historical Society, I, 1901, pp. 406–407*

Sunday the 27th [March, 1742/3] fair. I went to Town to Meeting to hear Mr Davenport, but it was Scarcely worth the hearing. the praying was without form or Comelyness. it was dificult to distinguish between his praying & preaching for it was all Meer Confused medley. he had no Text nor Bible visable, no Doctrine, uses, nor Improvement nor anything Else that was Regular forenoon Nor afternoon and the Last Sabath before by Report was of ye Same piece tho not on the Same Subject for then it was the hand of the Lord is upon me over & over many times; then Leave of & begin again the Same words verbatim. now it was (in addition to telling of his own Revelation & others Concerning the Shepherds Tent & other Such things) he Calld the people to Sing a New Song &c forevermore 30 or 40 times Imediately folowing as fast as one word could follow after another 30 or 40 times or more & yn Something Else & then over with it again. I cant Relate the Inconsistance of it. Monday 28 fair & very Cold. I stayed att brother Salmons all day & the Next. this week att So-hold & Next att Easthampton. & Southampton & Round the monday after from

Easthampton & Brothr Salmons. Mond 6. I Stayed at So-hold
till monday night 21s & yn Set out for oysterponds. very Cold
& Windy. I Lodged Brother Bayleys & Next night att deacon
Tuthills & 2 nights att Patience Beebees and on fryday 25th
I got over with James Beebee for 52s 6d our mony 15 in theirs
to mr John Champlins beforenoon, & then home. I Caryed my
great Horse & brot him over. I Lent to Mr Silvester my Lex
Testamentarian or Book of Wills. I Lodged at his house one
night as I went to Easthampton. Since I went Joseph Caulk-
ing hath Lost 2 Children Willm Newport on & an Infant of
Jonat Culvers & a Negro man of Jonathan Prenttis Sambo.
Saturd 26 fair & moderate cloudy. I was at home all day. wee
killed a hog Wt 190. Sund 27 fair & moderate. Mr adams pr
& I heard (a full Congregation) all Day. Mond 28 it Rained
the forepart of the Day. I was at home all Day. Tuesd 29 fair
Cold & Windy. I was at hom foren. aftern up to John Boles's
& John Prenttis's farm yt was Hamiltons about Conecting an
Encroachment on the Highway or Road. ye Committee & Se-
lectmen were there al night. Wednsd 30 Cold fair & windy.
I was up to John Rogers his farm helping Divide the fence between him & John Boles. itt is 1200 Rod from the Road to the
River Jno Prents West End 100 Rod & also between John Boles &
Sd Prenttis from the Road East & South John Boles ye west End
69 Rod & 9 Inches turning his N E Cornner 2 R & 10 foot. Jno
Prenttis as much South to a Cross fence. aftern I went to mr
adams's &c. there was mr Williams of Lebanon & Mr Edwards
of Northampton who with mr Lord of Norwich mr me-
cham of Coventry & pumroy of Hebron & Bellame of Woodbury and young Buel and Rosseter all come to Settle the disorders that are Subsisting among those Called New Lights
which follow Mr Davenport and Curtiss & allin &c. Thursd 31
fair till night & then Snow near ancle Deep. I had a Court about
burning Books on the 6h of March Curtice allin Tutthill
Sweasey Hill Shapley & C. Chris. adjourned to ye Courthouse
2 Clock where was the house full of People itt being Soon
after a Lecture Sermon pr by Mr Edwards of Northampton

very Suitable for the times to bear Wittness against ye prevailing disorders & destractions yt are Subsisting in the Country by means of Enthusiasm.

FRANCES MANWARING CAULKINS
History of New London, Connecticut. From the First Survey of the Coast in 1612, to 1860.

New London, 1895, 456–457

At a Court held in New London, in the county of New London March 31st, 1743, and continued by adjournment to the 5th of April, 1743. Present J. Hempstead justice of the Peace.

John Curtiss, Timothy Allen, Christopher Christophers, Daniel Shapley, Tuthill, and Sweasy being arrested and brought before this Court (upon the presentment of one of the grand-jurors of our Lord the King) to answer to the complaint exhibited against them, for that the persons aforesaid did on the 6th day of March instant, being Sabbath or Lord's Day gather themselves together with divers other persons unknown, (being some of them inhabitants of New London, and some of them transient persons) in the Town Street in New London aforesaid, near the dwelling-house of Edward Robinson of New London, and being so gathered together did there and then profane said day by kindling a fire in or near the street aforesaid and by throwing into said fire sundry good and useful treatises, books of practical godliness, the works of able divines, and whilst said books were consuming in the flames, did shout, hollow and scream, &c. (as per writ dated March 29th, 1743.)

And the parties defend; say they are not guilty; and for plea say that they are members of a Society allowed by the Statutes of William and Mary in the first year of their reign to worship God according to their own consciences, in a way different from that established in, and by the laws of this Colony and were most of them qualified at the County Court in this County before the day aforesaid, according to said statutes, and the rest were by then called to assist as teachers and persons to join in worship with said Society; that on the day mentioned in the writ, they all with many others were assembled for worship accordingly and that they in their consciences were then persuaded that heretical books in their custody ought publicly to be burned, that they accordingly burned those they thought to be such, that the same was solemnized with prayer, and singing praises to God, and that nothing in itself immoral was committed by them therein — that in the burning, praying and singing in such their separate society, was what they then judged in their consciences *Duty* and agreeable to the word of God, Acts 19, 19, and is the same mentioned in the writ, and no other things were done, nor with other view or motive.

The case is considered, and it is the opinion of this Court that they are all of them severally guilty of the profanation of the Sabbath, or Lord's Day, contrary to the laws of this Colony, and therefore give judgment that they the said John Curtis, &c., pay a fine of five shillings each and the cost of prosecution; taxed at £1, 18s, and 8d, to be proportionately paid between them, being 6s, 5⅓d, each, Old Tenor. In Lawful money the fine for each is 15d, and the part of the charge to each 1 shilling 7¼d.

C. Christophers paid his part in Court, and John Curtis to constable Burch.

Gentlemen's Progress: The Itinerarium of Dr. Alexander Hamilton, 1774, Carl Bridenbaugh, ed.

Chapel Hill, University of North Carolina Press for the Institute of Early American History and Culture, 1948, pp. 160–161

I left Williams's about half an hour after 3, and crossing the ferry a little after 5 o'clock, I arrived att New London and put up att Duchand's att the Sign of the Anchor. I did not know till now that I had any relations in this town; a parcell of children, as I rid up the lane, saluted me with "How d'ye unkle? Welcome to town, uncle."

Sunday, August 26, [1744]. I stayed att home most of the forenoon and was invited to dine with Collector Lechmere, son to the surveyor att Boston. . . .

I went home att 6 o'clock, and Deacon Green's son came to see me. He entertained me with the history of the behaviour of one Davenport, a fanatick preacher there who told his flock in one of his enthusiastic rhapsodies that in order to be saved they ought to burn all their idols. They began this conflagration with a pile of books in the public street, among which were Tillotson's Sermons, Beveridge's Thoughts, Drillincourt on Death, Sherlock and many other excellent authors, and sung psalms and hymns over the pile while it was a burning. They did not stop here, but the women made up a lofty pile of hoop petticoats, silk gowns, short cloaks, cambrick caps, red heeld shoes, fans, necklaces, gloves and other such aparrell, and what was merry enough, Davenport's own idol with which he topped the pile, was a pair of old, wore out, plush breaches. But this bone fire was happily prevented by one more moderate than the rest, who found means to perswade them that making such a sacrifice was not necessary for their salvation, and so every one carried of[f] their idols again, which was lucky for Davenport, who, had fire been put to the pile, would have been obliged to strutt about bare-arsed, for the devil another pair of breeches had he but these same old plush ones which were going to be offered up as an expiatory sacrifise. Mr. Green took his leave of me att 10 o'clock, and I went to bed.

JOSEPH TRACY
A History of the Revival of Religion in the Time of Edwards and Whitefield.

Boston, 1842, pp. 249–252

THE REV. MR. DAVENPORT'S REACTIONS

Although I do not question at all, but there is great reason to bless God for a glorious and wonderful work of his power and grace in the edification of his children, and the conviction and conversion of numbers in New England, in the neighbouring governments and several other parts, within a few years past; and believe that the Lord hath favored me, though most unworthy, with several others of his servants, in granting special assistance and success; the glory of all which be given to Jehovah, to whom alone it belongs:

Yet, after frequent meditation and desires that I might be enabled to apprehend things justly, and, I hope I may say, mature consideration, I am now fully convinced and persuaded that several appendages to this glorious work are no essential parts thereof, but of a different and contrary nature and tendency; which appendages I have been in the time of the work very industrious in, and instrumental of promoting, by a misguided zeal: being further much influenced in the affair by the false Spirit; which, unobserved by me, did (as I have been brought to see since) prompt me to unjust apprehensions and misconduct in several articles; which have been great blemishes to the work of God, very grievous to some of God's children, no less ensnaring and corrupting to others of them, a sad means of many persons' questioning the work of God, concluding and appearing against it, and of the hardening of multitudes in their sins, and an awful occasion of the enemies blaspheming the right ways of the Lord; and withal very offensive to that God, before whom I would lie in the dust, prostrate in deep humility and repentance on this account, imploring pardon for the Mediator's sake, and thankfully accepting the tokens thereof.

The articles which I especially refer to, and would in the most public manner retract, and warn others against, are these which follow, viz.

I. The method I used, for a considerable time, with respect to some, yea many ministers in several parts, in openly exposing such as I feared or thought unconverted, in public prayer or otherwise; herein making my private judgment, (in which also I much suspect I was mistaken in several instances, and I believe also that my judgment concerning several was formed rashly and upon very slender grounds,) I say, making my private judgment, the ground of public actions or conduct; offending, as I apprehend (although in the time of it, ignorantly) against the ninth commandment, and such other passages of Scripture as are similar; yea, I may say, offending against the laws both of justice and charity; which laws were further broken.

II. By my advising and urging to such separations from those ministers whom I treated as above, as I believe may be justly called rash, unwarrantable, and of sad and awful tendency and consequence. And here I would ask the forgiveness of those ministers, whom I have injured in both these articles.

III. I confess I have been much led astray by following impulses or impressions as a rule of conduct, whether they came with or without a text of Scripture; and my neglecting, also, duly to observe the analogy of Scripture. I am persuaded this was a great means of corrupting my experiences and carrying me off from the word of God, and a great handle, which the false Spirit has made use of with respect to a number, and me especially.

IV. I believe, further, that I have done much hurt to religion, by encouraging private persons to a ministerial and authoritative kind or method of exhorting; which is particularly observable in many, such being much puffed up and falling into the snare of the devil, whilst many others are thus directly prejudiced against the work.

I have reason to be deeply humbled that I have not been duly careful to endeavour to remove or prevent prejudice, (where I now believe I might then have done it consistently with duty,) which appeared remarkable in the method I practised, of singing with others in the streets, in societies frequently.

I would also penitently confess and bewail my great stiffness in retaining these aforesaid errors a great while, and unwillingness to examine into them with any jealousy of their being errors, notwithstanding the friendly counsels and cautions of real friends, especially in the ministry.

Here may properly be added a paragraph or two, taken out of a letter from me to Mr. Barber at Georgia; a true copy of which I gave consent, should be published lately at Philadelphia: '— I would add to what brother T—— hath written on the awful affair of books and clothes at New London, which affords grounds of deep and lasting humiliation; I was, to my shame be it spoken, the ringleader in that horrid action; I was, my dear brother, under the powerful influence of the false Spirit, almost one whole day together, and part of several days. The Lord showed me afterwards, that the spirit I was then acted by, was in its operations void of true inward peace, laying the greatest stress on externals, neglecting the heart, full of impatience, pride and arrogance; although I thought, in the time of it, that it was the Spirit of God in a high degree; awful, indeed! my body, especially my leg, much disordered at the same time,[1] which Satan and my evil heart might make some handle of.'

And now may the holy, wise and good God be pleased to guard and secure me against such errors for the future, and stop the progress of those, whether ministers or people, who have been corrupted by my words or example in any of the above mentioned particulars; and, if it be his holy will, bless this public recantation to this purpose. And O! may he grant, withal, that such, as by reason of the aforesaid errors and misconduct, have entertained unhappy prejudices against Christianity in general, or the late glorious work of God in particular, may, by this account, learn to distinguish the appendage from the substance or essence, that which is vile and odious, from that which is precious, glorious and divine, and thus be entirely and happily freed from all those prejudices referred to, and this, in infinite mercy through Jesus Christ: and to these requests, may all God's children, whether ministers or others, say Amen.

JAMES DAVENPORT.

July 28, 1744.

---

[1] "I had the long fever on me and the cankry humor, raging at once."

P.S. Inasmuch as a number, who have fallen in with and promoted the aforesaid errors and misconduct, and are not altered in their minds, may be prejudiced against this Recantation, by a supposition or belief, that I came into it by reason of desertion or dullness and deadness in religion, it seems needful, therefore, to signify, what I hope I may say without boasting, and what I am able, through pure rich grace, to speak with truth and freedom, that for some months in the time of my coming to the abovesaid conclusions and retractions, and since I have come through grace to them, I have been favored, a great part of the time, with a sweet calm and serenity of soul, and rest in God, and sometimes with special and remarkable refreshments of soul, and these more free from corrupt mixtures than formerly. Glory to God alone. J. D.

Although most Americans responded initially in a favorable manner to the revival, by 1743 many felt that the phenomenon's "errors and disorders" indicated clearly that it was not the work of God but of the devil. Meetings of proponents ("New Lights") and opponents ("Old Lights") of the revival in New England produced public testimonies which offer a view of the positions taken by each side in the great debate.

JOSEPH TRACY
A History of the Revival of Religion in the Time of Edwards and Whitefield.
Boston, 1842, pp. 287–288, 295–299

The TESTIMONY of the Pastors of the Churches in the Province of Massachusetts Bay, in New England, at their Annual Convention in Boston, May 25, 1743, against several Errors in Doctrine and Disorders in Practice, which have of late obtained in various Parts of the Land; as drawn up by a Committee chosen by the said Pastors, read and accepted, paragraph by paragraph, and voted to be signed by the Moderator in their name, and printed.

We, the pastors of the churches of Christ in the province of Massachusetts Bay, in New England, at our Annual Convention, May 25, 1743, taking into consideration several errors in doctrine and disorders in practice that have of late obtained in various parts of the land, look upon ourselves bound, in duty to our great Lord and Master, Jesus Christ, and in concern for the purity and welfare of these churches, in the most public manner to bear our testimony against them.

I. As to errors in doctrine; we observe that some in our land look upon what are called secret impulses upon their minds, without due regard to the written word, the rule of their conduct; that none are converted but such as know they are converted, and the time when; that assurance is of the essence of saving faith; that sanctification is no evidence of justification; with other Antinomian and Familistical errors which flow from these; all which, as we judge, are contrary to the pure doctrines of the Gospel, and testified against and confuted in the Acts of the Synod of August, 1637; as printed in a book entitled "The Rise, and Reign, and Ruin, of Antinomianism, &c., in New England."

II. As to disorders in practice, we judge,

1. The itinerancy, as it is called, by which either ordained ministers or young candidates go from place to place, and without the knowledge, or contrary to the leave of the stated pastors in such places, assemble their people to hear themselves preach, — arising, we fear, from too great an opinion of themselves, and an uncharitable opinion of those pastors, and a want of faith in the great Head of the churches, is a breach of order, and contrary to the Scriptures, 1 Pet. 4: 15; 2 Cor. 10: 12, to the end, and the sentiments of our fathers expressed in their Platform of Church Discipline, chap. 9, sect. 6.

2. Private persons of no education and but low attainments in knowledge and in the great doctrines of the gospel, without any regular call, under a pretence of exhorting, taking upon themselves to be preachers of the word of God, we judge to be a heinous invasion of the ministerial office, offensive to God, and destructive to these churches; contrary to Scripture, Numb. 16: 1 Cor. 28, 29, and testified against in a "Faithful Advice to the Churches of New England" by several of our venerable fathers.

3. The ordaining or separating of any persons to the work of the evangelical ministry at large, and without any relation to a particular charge, which some of late have unhappily gone into, we look upon as contrary to the Scriptures, and directly opposite to our Platform, chap. 6. sect, 3, and the practice of the Protestant churches; as may be seen in "The order of the Churches Vindicated," by the very Reverend Dr. Increase Mather.

4. The spirit and practice of separation from the particular flocks to which persons belong, to join themselves with, and support lay exhorters or itinerants, is very subversive of the churches of Christ, opposite to the rule of the gospel, Gal. 5: 19, 20; Jude 19; 1 Cor. 12: 25; 1 Cor. 3: 3, and utterly condemned by our Platform, chap. 13, sect. 1, 5, and contrary to their covenant engagements.

5. Persons assuming to themselves the prerogatives of God, to look into and judge the hearts of their neighbours, censure and condemn their brethren, especially their ministers, as Pharisees, Arminians, blind and unconverted, &c., when their doctrines are agreeable to the gospel and their lives to their Christian profession, is, we think, most contrary to the spirit and precepts of the gospel and the example of Christ, and highly unbecoming the character of those who call themselves the disciples of the meek and lowly Jesus. John 13: 34, 35; 1 Sam. 16: 7; Mat. 7: 1; Rom. 14: 10.

6. Though we deny not that the human mind, under the operations of the Divine Spirit, may be overborne with terrors and joys; yet the many confusions that have appeared in some places, from the vanity of mind and ungoverned passions of people, either in the excess of sorrow or joy, with the disorderly tumults and indecent behaviour of persons, we judge to be so far from an indication of the special presence of God with those preachers that have industriously excited and countenanced them, or in the assemblies where they prevail, that they are a plain evidence of the weakness of human nature; as the history of the enthusiasms that have appeared in the world, in several ages, manifests. Also, I Cor. 14: 23, 40. At the same time we

bear our testimony against the impious spirit of those that from hence take occasion to reproach the work of the Divine Spirit in the hearts of the children of God.

Upon the whole, we earnestly recommend the churches of this country to the gracious care and conduct of the great Shepherd of the sheep, with our thankful acknowledgments for his merciful regard to them in supplying them with faithful pastors, and protecting them from the designs of their enemies, and advancing his spiritual kingdom in the souls of so many, from the foundation of this country to this day; and where there is any special revival of pure religion in any parts of our land at this time, we would give unto God all the glory. And we earnestly advise all our brethren in the ministry carefully to endeavour to preserve their churches pure in their doctrine, discipline and manners, and guard them against the intrusion of itinerants and exhorters, to uphold a spirit of love towards one another, and all men; which, together with their fervent prayers, will be the most likely means, under God, to promote the true religion of the holy Jesus, and hand it, uncorrupt, to succeeding generations .

> *Signed,*
>
> NATHANIEL EELLS, *Moderator,*
>
> *in the name and by order of the Convention.*

The Testimony and Advice of an Assembly of Pastors of Churches in New England, at a meeting in Boston, July 7, 1743, occasioned by the late happy Revival Religion in many parts of the Land.

If it is the duty of every one capable of observation and reflection, to take a constant religious notice of what occurs in the daily course of common providence; how much more is it expected that those events in the divine economy, wherein there is a signal display of the power, grace and mercy of God in behalf of the church, should be observed with sacred wonder, pleasure, and gratitude! Nor should the people of God content themselves with a silent notice, but publish with the voice of thanksgiving, and tell of all his wondrous works.

More particularly, when Christ is pleased to come into his church in a plentiful effusion of his Holy Spirit, by whose powerful influences the ministration of the word is attended with uncommon success, salvation-work carried on in an eminent manner, and his kingdom, which is within men, and consists in righteousness and peace and joy in the Holy Ghost, is notably advanced, this is an event which, above all others, invites the notice and bespeaks the praises of the Lord's people, and should be declared abroad for a memorial of the divine grace; as it tends to confirm the divinity of a despised gospel, and manifests the work of the Holy Spirit in the application of redemption, which too many are ready to reproach; as it may have a happy effect, by the divine blessing, for the revival of religion in other places, and the enlargement of the kingdom of Christ in the world; and as it tends to enliven the prayers, strengthen the faith, and raise the hopes, of such as are waiting for the kingdom of God, and the coming on of the glory of the latter days.

But if it is justly expected of all who profess themselves the disciples of Christ, that they should openly acknowledge and rejoice in a work of this nature, wherein the honor of their divine Master is so much concerned; how much more is it to be looked for from those who are employed in the ministry of the Lord Jesus, and so stand in a special relation to him, as servants of his household, and officers in his kingdom! These stand as watchmen upon the walls of Jerusalem; and it is their business not only to give the alarm of war when the enemy is approaching, but to sound the trumpet of praise when the King of Zion cometh, in a meek triumph, having salvation.

For these and other reasons, we, whose names are hereunto annexed, pastors of churches in New England, met together in Boston, July 7, 1743, think it our indispensable duty, (without judging or censuring such of our brethren as cannot at present

see things in the same light with us,) in this open and conjunct
manner to declare, to the glory of sovereign grace, our full
persuasion, either from what we have seen ourselves, or received
upon credible testimony, that there has been a happy and remarkable revival of religion in many parts of this land, through
an uncommon divine influence; after a long time of great decay
and deadness, and a sensible and very awful withdraw of the
Holy Spirit from his sanctuary among us.

Though the work of grace wrought on the hearts of men by
the word and Spirit of God, and which has been more or less
carried on in the church from the beginning, is always the same
for substance, and agrees, at one time and another, in one place
or person and another, as to the main strokes and lineaments
of it, yet the present work appears to be remarkable and extraordinary,

On account of the numbers wrought upon. We never before
saw so many brought under soul concern, and with distress
making the inquiry, What must we do to be saved? And these
persons of all characters and ages. *With regard to the sudden-
ness and quick progress of it.* Many persons and places were
surprised with the gracious visit together, or near about the
same time; and the heavenly influence diffused itself far and
wide like the light of the morning. *Also in respect of the degree of operation*, both in a way of terror and in a way of consolation; attended in many with unusual bodily effects.

Not that all who are accounted the subjects of the present
work, have had these extraordinary degrees of previous distress
and subsequent joy. But many, and we suppose the greater
number, have been wrought on in a more gentle and silent way,
and without any other appearances than are common and usual
at other times, when persons have been awakened to a solemn
concern about salvation, and have been thought to have passed
out of a state of nature into a state of grace.

As to those whose inward concern has occasioned extraordinary outward distresses, the most of them, when we came to
converse with them, were able to give, what appeared to us, a

rational account of what so affected their minds; viz., a quick sense of their guilt, misery, and danger; and they would often mention the passages in the sermons they heard, or particular texts of Scripture, which were set home upon them with such a powerful impression. And as to such whose joys have carried them into transports and extasies, they in like manner have accounted for them, from a lively sense of the danger they hoped they were freed from, and the happiness they were now possessed of; such clear views of divine and heavenly things, and particularly of the excellencies and loveliness of Jesus Christ, and such sweet tastes of redeeming love, as they never had before. The instances were very few in which we had reason to think these affections were produced by visionary or sensible representations, or by any other images than such as the Scripture itself presents unto us.

And here we think it not amiss to declare, that in dealing with these persons, we have been careful to inform them, that the nature of conversion does not consist in these passionate feelings; and to warn them not to look upon their state safe, because they have passed out of deep distress into high joys, unless they experience a renovation of nature, followed with a change of life, and a course of vital holiness. Nor have we gone into such an opinion of the bodily effects with which this work has been attended in some of its subjects, as to judge them any signs that persons who have been so affected, were then under a saving work of the Spirit of God. No; we never so much as called these bodily seisures, convictions; or spake of them as the immediate work of the Holy Spirit. Yet we do not think them inconsistent with a work of God upon the soul at that very time; but judge that those inward impressions which come from the Spirit of God, those terrors and consolations of which he is the author, may, according to the natural frame and constitution which some persons are of, occasion such bodily effects; and therefore that those extraordinary outward symptoms are not an argument that the work is delusive, or from the influence and agency of the evil spirit.

With respect to numbers of those who have been under the impressions of the present day, we must declare there is good ground to conclude they are become real Christians; the account they give of their conviction and consolation agreeing with the standard of the Holy Scriptures, corresponding with the experiences of the saints, and evidenced by the external fruits of holiness in their lives; so that they appear to those who have the nearest access to them, as so many epistles of Christ, written, not with ink, but by the Spirit of the living God, attesting to the genuineness of the present operation, and representing the excellency of it.

Indeed, many, who appeared to be under convictions, and were much altered in their external behaviour when this work began, and while it was most flourishing, have lost their impressions, and are relapsed into their former manner of life. Yet of those who were judged hopefully converted, and made a public profession of religion, there have been fewer instances of scandal and apostasy than might be expected. So that, as far as we are able to form a judgment, the face of religion is lately changed much for the better in many of our towns and congregations; and together with a reformation observable in divers instances, there appears to be more experimental godliness and lively Christianity, than the most of us can remember we have ever seen before.

Thus we have freely declared our thoughts as to the work of God, so remarkably revived in many parts of this land. And now, we desire to bow the knee in thanksgiving to the God and Father of our Lord Jesus Christ, that our eyes have seen and our ears heard such things. And while these are our sentiments, we must necessarily be grieved at any accounts sent abroad, representing this work as all enthusiasm, delusion and disorder.

Indeed, it is not to be denied, that in some places many irregularities and extravagances have been permitted to accompany it, which we would deeply lament and bewail before God, and look upon ourselves obliged, for the honor of the Holy Spirit, and of his blessed operations on the souls of men, to bear a public and faithful testimony against; though at the same time it is to be acknowledged with much thankfulness, that in other places, where the work has greatly flourished, there have been few, if any, of these disorders and excesses. But who can wonder, if at such a time as this, Satan should intermingle himself, to hinder and blemish a work so directly contrary to the interests of his own kingdom? Or if, while so much good seed is sowing, the enemy should be busy to sow tares? We would therefore, in the bowels of Jesus, beseech such as have been partakers of this work, or are zealous to promote it, that they be not ignorant of Satan's devices; that they watch and pray against errors and misconduct of every kind, lest they blemish and hinder that which they desire to honor and advance. Particularly,

That they do not make secret impulses on their minds, without a due regard to the written word, the rule of their duty: a very dangerous mistake, which, we apprehend, some in these times have gone into. That to avoid Arminianism, they do not verge to the opposite side of Antinomianism; while we would have others take good heed to themselves, lest they be by some led into, or fixed in, Arminian tenets, under the pretense of opposing Antinomian errors. That laymen do not invade the ministerial office, and, under a pretense of exhorting, set up preaching; which is very contrary to gospel order, and tends to introduce errors and confusion into the church. That ministers do not invade the province of others, and in ordinary cases preach in another's parish without his knowledge, and against his consent; nor encourage raw and indiscreet young candidates, in rushing into particular places, and preaching publicly or privately, as some have done, to the no small disrepute and damage of the work in places where it once promised to flourish. Though at the same time we would have ministers show their regard to the spiritual welfare of their people, by suffering them to partake of the gifts and graces of able, sound and zealous

preachers of the word, as God in his providence may give opportunity therefor; being persuaded God has in this day remarkably blessed the labors of some of his servants who have
travelled in preaching the gospel of Christ. That people beware
of entertaining prejudices against their own pastors, and do not
run into unscriptural separations. That they do not indulge a
disputatious spirit, which has been attended with mischievous
effects; nor discover a spirit of censoriousness, uncharitableness,
and rash judging the state of others; than which scarce any
thing has more blemished the work of God amongst us. And
while we would meekly exhort both ministers and Christians,
so far as is consistent with truth and holiness, to follow the
things that make for peace; we would most earnestly warn all
sorts of persons not to despise these outpourings of the Spirit,
lest a holy God be provoked to withhold them, and instead
thereof, to pour out upon this people the vials of his wrath, in
temporal judgments and spiritual plagues; and would call upon
every one to improve this remarkable season of grace, and put in
for a share of the heavenly blessings so liberally dispensed.

Finally, we exhort the children of God to continue instant in
prayer, that He with whom is the residue of the Spirit, would
grant us fresh, more plentiful and extensive effusions, that so
this wilderness, in all the parts of it, may become a fruitful field;
that the present appearances may be an earnest of the glorious
things promised to the church in the latter days; when she shall
shine with the glory of the Lord arisen upon her, so as to dazzle
the eyes of beholders, confound and put to shame all her enemies, rejoice the hearts of her solicitous and now saddened
friends, and have a strong influence and resplendency throughout the earth. Amen! Even so. Come, Lord Jesus; come
quickly!

The division of the clergy over the revival soon filtered down to the level of individual churches and congregations, resulting in a good deal of conflict and schism. One such separation occurred in the First Church of Plymouth, Massachusetts. The issues are revealed in the following selections from the writings of pastor Nathaniel Leonard and of Josiah Cotton, one leader of opposition within the church.

The Christian History, Containing Accounts of the Revival and Propagation of Religion in Great Britain and America, Thomas Prince, Jr., ed.

Boston, 1743–1745, II, pp. 313–314

[*Nathaniel Leonard's Testimony*]

November 23, 1744

It pleased God to cast my lot (who am the least of all saints) in the First Church and town in the country, above twenty years ago. Religion was then under a great decay; most people seemed to be taken up principally about the world and the lusts of this life; though there appeared some serious Christians among us that had the things of God at heart, who greatly bewailed the growth of impiety, profaneness, Sabbath breaking, gaming, tavern haunting, intemperance, and other evils, which threatened to bear down all that is good and sacred before them. We were sensible of an awful degeneracy, and kept days of fasting and prayer, year after year, that God would pour out his Spirit upon us; especially on the rising generation. At these times we invited the ministers of the county to join with us, who readily gave their assistance. The authority of this town endeavoured to put a stop to the growing intemperance, by clearing the taverns at nine o'clock in the evening, and punishing loose and disorderly persons that frequented them. But all the methods used one way and the other, proved of little effect. Iniquity prevailed, and we were in danger of losing the very form of godliness.

The Rev. Mr. Whitefield coming into the land, and the news we presently had of his preaching and conversation at Boston and elsewhere, roused us a little, and we sent to him to come and preach to us. We expected him in October, 1740, but were disappointed.

In March following, the Rev. Mr. Tennent came hither and preached eight sermons to general acceptance, which, by the blessing of God, greatly awakened this people, and many have dated such religious impressions from that time, as we have reason to believe issued in a real conversion to God. After him, several ministers of the county and others visited us, and preached with us; and we often spent whole days in prayer, singing and preaching, and had frequently three exercises in them. I often preached three times on the Lord's day myself, and sometimes three or four times in the week besides; although before this, through bodily indisposition and heaviness of spirit, I was not able to carry on the usual stated exercises, and my people had for some years provided me an assistant.

The subjects chiefly insisted on were these following, viz.: The sin and apostasy of mankind in Adam; the blindness of the natural man in the things of God; the enmity of the carnal mind; the evil of sin; the desert of it, and the utter inability of the fallen creature to relieve itself; the sovereignty of God; his righteousness, holiness, truth, power, eternity; also his grace and mercy in Christ Jesus; the way of redemption by Christ; justification, through his imputed righteousness, received by faith; this faith the gift of God, and a living principle, that worketh by love; legal and evangelical repentance; the nature and necessity of regeneration; and that without holiness no man can see God. All persons were put upon examining themselves, warned against trusting in their own righteousness, and resting in the form of godliness, without the power, &c. These things, together with pathetical invitations to sinners, to come and embrace the Lord Jesus Christ as offered in the Gospel, made a wonderful impression on the minds of all sorts of people at the first. And men, women and children were much awakened, and the outward face of things began exceedingly to alter.

In February, 1742, the Rev. Mr. Croswell came hither, and
continued in the town about a fortnight, preaching sometimes
in this, and sometimes in the other parish. At this time, I think
I may say, as the apostle does to the Thessalonians: "The Gospel
came unto us, not in word only, but also in power, and in the
Holy Ghost, and in much assurance. And we received the
word, not as the word of man, but as it is in truth, the word of
God, which wrought effectually in them that believed." Hundreds of souls were at one time in the meetinghouse, Saturday,
February 13th, crying out in the utmost concern, what they
should do to be saved! and many others rejoicing in the Lord,
in the sweet sense of his redeeming love and grace in Christ
Jesus, as they declared. This day, and at some other times, conversions were so open and public, that we seemed to see souls,
dead in trespasses and sins, revive and stand up monuments of
divine grace. I do not mean that we had an intuition of their
hearts, and knew infallibly the state of their souls, which is
God's prerogative; but the appearance of conversion from one
state to the other, and the alteration in the frame and temper of
their minds, which they discovered in words and behaviour, was
admirable. This day appeared to me in the time of it, and hath
done so ever since, a day of great grace, for which my soul
giveth thanks to God.

After this, for some months together, you should scarcely
see any body at the taverns, unless they were strangers, travel-
lers, or some come there upon necessary business. The children
foresook their plays in the streets, and persons of all demonina-
tions, except a few, gave themselves to reading the word of
God, and other books of devotion, to meditation, prayer, conference, and other religious exercises, and refrained from their
customary vices. And many that lived at a distance, being acquainted with this town in its former state, coming hither,
beheld us now with admiration, saying, Surely the fear of God
is in this place.

Furthermore, as this present life is a state of imperfection,
so there were some circumstances that attended this work,

which, if they had not been, might have prevented some prejudice and offence against it.

A violent opposition presently arose, and prevailed so far,
that a number of this congregation went out from us into a distinct society, and nine of the brethren asked a dismission from
us, to embody into a church by themselves. We readily granted
their request, and they have lately had a minister set over them.
My prayer for him and them is, "that God would pour out his
Spirit abundantly upon them, greatly enrich them with heavenly blessings, and fill them with all the fulness of God."

As for the subjects of this work, it hath been here as in other
places. Some, that were a while under awakenings, at length got
rid of them, and are now returned as the dog to his vomit.
Some, that we thought at first savingly changed, have since
given reason to fear that they deceived themselves as well as
others. But the far greater part of them that were added to the
church, behave with such meekness, humility, sobriety, and
other Christian virtues, that I must say of them, as David did
of the godly of his day: "They are the excellent of the earth,
in whom is my delight." But I would not be understood to con-
fine my good opinion to those only that have passed under a
remarkable change within three or four years past. No, I am
persuaded there are a number of truly godly persons among us,
that experienced the new birth before these days, and even
before my settlement in this town, for whom I have an equal
regard.

As to the present state of religion, the town is much reformed
from what it was before these days. But Christians are not so
lively as they have been; the convincing Spirit seems in a great
measure withdrawn; iniquity begins to grow more bold of late;
and I am afraid a day of sore declension is coming upon this
place. O that God would again visit this vine, which his right
hand hath planted, and hath hitherto preserved! O that he
would water it every moment! Nothing but a stream of grace,
from that fountain where all fulness dwells, can maintain and
carry on a work of reformation against the devices of the

devil, the snares of the world, and the opposition of men's hearts.

I am so confirmed in it that this work is of God, that in my most calm and sedate seasons my prayer is, not only that God would lead me and guide me in his way, but enable me to endure all manner of ill usage in the world, rather than give up this cause, which I am fully persuaded is his, to whom be glory and praise for ever and ever. Amen.

JOSIAH COTTON

Memoirs containing Some Account of the Predecessors, Relations, Posterity & Alliances (with some remarkable Occurrencies in the Life and Circumstances) of Josiah Cotton of Plymouth in New-England, Esq. . . ."

Boston, *Manuscript in Massachusetts Historical Society,*
pp. 314–316, 334–335, 337, 342–343

Plym'o Die Saturnii Jan'ii 8th 1742/3

. . . On February 6 Mr. Croswell (that had been some time Minister at Monument Ponds in Plym'o, & now an ordained Minist'r at Groton in Connecticut Colony) arrived at Plymouth & on February 7 Sacrament Day Preacht P.M. on Matt. 11, 28, wherein he declared (as he did afterwards at Jones River) that he had reason to think ¾ of the Communicants of that day were unconverted. He preacht also at night, & the next night, & the day or night following, evedatly trying might & main to work upon the passions of the people whereby at length [they] begun to make a great noise & cry out as in distress, & Mr. Croswell declared the Spirit of the living God was come or coming down amongst them, & so went on from day to day preaching or exhorting till Saturday Feb'y 13 when the assembly came together about 11 o Clock before noon, some singing hymns as they came thro' the Streets (as was also done at other times) & being in the meeting house such was the noise thro distress & joy, real or pretended, that the Ministers neither preached nor prayed, but Mr Croswell went about the

Meeting house Crying mercy, mercy, mercy sufficient in the blood of Christ for the chief of Sinners & c. and in such a frame they continued till 9 at night that it is impossible to imagine except one had seen & heard it; and thus meetings were carried on not only in the Town but in the other Precinct at Monument Ponds, publickly or more privately, many times till 11 oClock at night or past, from the 9th of February till the 13 of March, Mr Leonard imitating Croswells managments after his departure to Charlestown which was about the begining of March last. Was the utmost confusion in their meetings, some Singing, some crying some laughing for Joy, others opposing &c, all at once, & the Pulpit filt with Boys & a Negro or two who were directed to invite others to come to Christ, particularly *old Grey headed Sinners* and all these Justifyed privately & publicly, & the holy Scriptures wrested to patronize the same. Several declaring they were Glorious things & times so that both Ministers & people seemed to filled with Enthusiasm, An hour or two in Distress, & then filled with Joy & assurance, wanting nothing but wings to fly directly to Heaven; whereas there seems a truth in that observation made by some, *That Faith which comes to perfection in its birth is a Monster.* The Consequences of these things where great addittons to the Church & something of a reformation, or rather alteration, for it is a doubt with me whether a change from open profaneness & irreligion to enthusiasm & rash Judging of others be a proper Judgmation, calling others that did not run the same length, & were for more order & decency Pharisees & opposers of the work of God &c. Whereby many became offended & troubled, some absented from the Sacrament, some went to other meetings or stayed at home, and things are go to that pass, that there seems to be a real design of seperating finally & erecting a new meeting house, by those who are dissatisfied at these unusual, unaccountable proceedings. And indeed it is not only in our town but generally throughout the Countrey, Trances, visions, & impulses, sway many & drive them hither & thither. . . .

Plym'o Die Dominico Jan'ii 8th 1743/4 . . . . The famous Mr. Edwards Minist'r of North Hampton, the Chief Writer of the New Thinkers (as some call them) has put forth a Book containing 300 & Pages, wherein he condemns many ill practices of the New Lights but with all is very positive, & labours might & main to prove the main of the work to be the work of God. And in Opposition thereto Doct'r Chauncey of Boston has put forth a larger Book to prove the main of the Work to be bad. — And thus we are Divided in Opinion which has Occasioned several Separate Assemblies at Plimouth, Boston, Newbury, Providence, &c. — Thô the Separation at Plimouth is different from the others for that is of the Old Lights from the New — About 80 men having Built a New-Meeting House which was Raised July 7th in King Street, partly because there had been so much Disorder in the Old One, and partly because it was an Old One and insufficient to Accommodate all the Inhabitants. Which New-Meeting House Dedicated and Devoted to the Publick Worship of God by the Rev'd Mr. Eells of Scituate who Preached on Psal. 84. 11 ver, a large Assembly being present on Thursday the fifth Instant. And he also preached in it the first Sabb'th the 8th of January &c — The Society that Built the New House (where I purchased a Pew) were upon their Petition Set off by the Precinct the beginning of Decem'r last. Several other Things Contained in s'd Petition, particularly That the Ministers of Each Assembly should be maintained by a Tax upon the whole &c, being denied by the Maj'r Part who have also Voted to pull down the Old Meeting House & to build a very large new one by Subscription. . . . Altho disorders at religious meetings are almost wholly ceased among us Yet some stumbling Blocks remain. As 1. That never any sufficient publick testimony has been here born against such disorders. 2. That Itinerant preaching is too much allowed & incouraged. 3. That numbers are too harshly admitted into the Church without doing due pennance for notorious faults as we suppose. . . .

Plym'o Die Martes Jan'ii 8th 1744/5 . . . . On May 25 there was
a fast day kept in the new meeting house about getting a Minister. Mr. Angier preached a. m. upon Jno. 15. 7 & Mr Eells
P.M. on 2 Cor. 6 pt. 16 v — Ye are the Temple of the Living
God & at the same time a small Church gathered. The Ministers
that were nominated for probation amongst us were Mr. Ste-
vens, Mr Marsh, Mr. Adams, the three last came upon tryal
after the nomination, but the people not being well agreed,
agreed to send for another viz. Mr. Thomas Frink who had
been a settled Minister at Rutland in the County of Worcester
for some years past but parted from his people, & he accepting
the invitation came & in about 5 Weeks came (was as it were)
unanimously chosen, tho for my part I thought the Choice so
sudden & hasty that I could not join in it. Howsoever in about
a weeks time he accepted of the Call & his installment being
appointed on the 7th of Nov'r it was accordingly attended.
Doctor Chauncey of Boston preached the Sermon, on 2 Tim:
4.16, Mr. Eells gave the Charge, & Mr Loring of Sudbury gave
the Right Hand of Fellowship &c. Of this Gentleman I had
this Character in a Letter, dated from Boston Oct'r 19. That
he was a very good Preacher an excellent Scholar, of great
Reading & strong powers, tho of a pretty high Temper &c.
I pray God he may be an instrument of much good to many
Souls. January 7 — They proceed to the Choice of Deacon,
which were Mr. Samuel Nelson & Capt'n Josiah Carver. Doct'r
Chauncey in his Sermon (which was a very good one &
printed) advised & exhorted Ministers not to admit Itinerant
preachers into their Pulpits, & especially that Grand one &c the
beginner of it, who was again lately arrived in Countrey &c.
not naming but describing Mr. Whitfield, but alas! it will have
a different turn (with many) from what he intended, for all
the Doct'rs in the Countrey cant make a plaister that will Cure
itching Ears. . . .

Many of the proponents of the revival went a good deal further than Nathaniel Leonard of Plymouth or the July, 1743, Testimony in their support. Some converts, particularly those in eastern Connecticut, carried their new-found religious zeal to its logical conclusions and insisted upon translating their revival experiences into doctrinal and ecclesiastical principles. This led them to break away from the "corrupt" churches in which they had been brought up and to found new "correct" ones, following the biblical injunction to "come ye out and be ye separate;" hence these ecclesiastical radicals earned the name "Separates." Their beliefs are revealed in the following dialogue between several Separate leaders in Canterbury, Connecticut, and a ministerial candidate being interviewed for a permanent position.

ELLEN D. LARNED
History of Windham Country, Connecticut, I.
Worcester, 1874, pp. 405–406

CANTERBURY, *Sep.* 7, *1743.*

To the Church of Christ now met by adjournment: —

Dearly Beloved: According to your order, we, the subscribers, waited upon Mr. Adams, informed him that the church was dissatisfied, and gave him a copy of the church's vote concerning his sermons, I. Cor. x: 31, and in answer to what the church saith of the general run of said sermons (in that they imply that man hath a power to glorify God, not implying that the new birth is necessary) he saith, 'That he was preaching to Christians, and they had passed through the new birth, and therefore it was not needful to show the necessity of it.' We asked him, 'Whether he thought that all who heard him were such?'

ADAMS. 'No! but all that I directed my discourse to were.'

COM. 'It did not appear so by the terms used in addressing them.'

A. 'In opening the text, I did show that the Apostle writ to the Christians at Corinth, and that showed that I was preaching to Christians. Is not that true?'

C. 'It is true the *Apostle* did as you say, but in your doctrine, the foundation of your discourse, you address them under the general denomination of men, which is not peculiar to Christians, but when it is used by way of distinction it denotes men in their natural estate.'

A. 'Women heard me, too, and you may say I did not preach to *them* because I did not call them women.'

C. 'Preaching up duty and works as terms of life is dangerous.'

A. 'I did not say they were terms of life but what Christians ought to do because they were redeemed, which I laid down as an obligation to obedience, and also showed that I was showing Christians their duty, and ought they not to do those duties that I laid down?'

C. 'Many of them were duties that ought to be done, and the doing of them to be pressed upon Christians, but you did not show that faith in Jesus Christ and the love of God in the soul were absolutely necessary in order to glorify God in doing them.'

A. 'I did mention faith and love, with several other things, as necessary.'

C. 'But inasmuch as you pat them with several other things, and then said that all or some of them were necessary, you so left it in your sermon that people might take the other and leave out faith and love, as not being so absolutely necessary.'

A. 'I could not help that, and nobody would take my sermons as the church hath represented, except they were prejudiced against me.'

C. 'Some that like your preaching *have* taken it so, and say they are of opinion that if a man doth what he can he shall be accepted.'

A. 'You need not fear it hurting *you, knowing you are converted* as you say.'

C. 'Our hearts are so apt to deceive us on that point, we earnestly desire to have the Word divided aright after we have been enlightened and sanctified in part, but we look upon it most dangerous for those poor souls that are dead in sins, for they know of no other way but to do and live. . . . One of us was discoursing with a man in this town concerning that point, and the man said, "That God doth not require anything of any man but what he hath given power to do." '

A. 'It *is* true that God hath given him power to do all that he requires of him.'

COM. 'Has God given every man power to believe?'

A. 'Was any man ever lost who did what he could to save himself, or towards his own salvation?'

When he had heard what he, as above-written, saith to the general expression the church had taken, we then discoursed of the particulars that were in themselves contrary to sound doctrine, viz., that it is not necessary in every particular to . . . [*illegible*] . . . the Glory of God, and he, to rectifie that point asked, 'Whether perfect sinless obedience was required under the Gospel?'

COM. 'Nothing but a perfect righteousness would be accepted.'

A. 'We are not under the Law, but under Grace.'

COM. 'Shall we continue in sin because we are not under the Law?'

A. 'No. But would you have me preach that man must have a perfect sinless obedience?'

COM. 'They must aim at and endeavor after it, but it is in their aims that you have left such room, and that makes it the more dangerous, and in your saying that it matters not much whether a man knows precisely whether the reward of happiness or the glory of God be the chief motive to put him upon doing, &c., we look upon it to be the more dangerous, because we are of opinion that that is the most necessary and most difficult point to know in self-examination.'

A. 'What goes before and follows after in my sermon guards against this danger.'

Com. 'You have not said anything in your sermons that implied that there were any that were in danger of perishing in the state they were in.'

A. 'I did, in showing how they should come to God, imply that as plainly as if I had said it in plain words.'

Com. 'But you did not tell them they had no legs nor power to come, and they were dead.'

A. 'Christians have legs, and such I was preaching to.'

We informed him that the church would meet on this day, and we desired him to be present at this meeting. He said he was going out of town. We asked him what answer we should give the church on the premises. He said, he cared not what, and left us.

Solomon Paine
Thomas Bradford
Benajah Douglas.

Public response to George Whitefield's preaching tour of 1739–1741 was most enthusiastic in New England and the Middle Colonies; the Southern Colonies remained virtually oblivious to revival until somewhat later. The sequence in the South is suggested in Samuel Davies' account of the coming of the revival to Virginia.

JOSEPH TRACY

A History of the Revival of Religion in the Time of Edwards and Whitefield.

Boston, 1842, pp. 377–384

[*Samuel Davies to Joseph Bellamy, June 28, 1751*]

I have prevailed, Sir, on my good friend before mentioned, who was the principal private instrument of promoting the late work, and therefore well acquainted with it, to write me a narrative of its rise and progress from this period till my settlement here; and this, together with the substance of what he and others

have told me, I shall present to you without any material altera-
tions, and personate him, though I shall not exactly use his words.

"The Rev. Mr. Whitefield had been in Virginia, I think, in the
year 1740, and at the invitation of the Rev. Mr. Blair, our late
Commissary, had preached in Williamsburg, our metropolis,
about sixty miles from Hanover. His fame was much spread
abroad, as a very warm and alarming preacher; which made
such of us in Hanover as had been awakened, very eager to see
and hear him; but as he left the colony before we heard of him,
we had no opportunity. But in the year 1743, a young gentleman arrived from Scotland with a book of his sermons preached
in Glasgow, and taken from his mouth in short hand, which
with difficulty I procured. After I had read it with great liking
and benefit, I invited my neighbors to come and hear it; and
the plainness, popularity and fervency of the discourses being
peculiarly fitted to affect our unimproved minds, and the Lord
rendering the word efficacious, many were convinced of their
undone condition, and constrained to seek deliverance with the
greatest solicitude. A considerable number convened every
Sabbath to hear these sermons, instead of going to church, and
frequently on week days. The concern of some was so passionate and violent, that they could not avoid crying out, weeping
bitterly, &c., and that when such indications of religious concern were so strange and ridiculous, that they could not be
occasioned by example or sympathy, and the affectation of
them would have been so unprofitable an instance of hypocrisy,
that none could be tempted to it. My dwellinghouse at length
was too small to contain the people; whereupon we determined
to build a meetinghouse, merely for reading; for we knew of
no minister in the world whom we could get to preach to us
according to our liking; and having never been accustomed to
social extempore prayer, none of us durst attempt it in company. By this single mean, sundry were solemnly awakened, and
their conduct ever since is a living attestation of the continuance
and happy issue of their impressions. When the report of these
sermons and the effects occasioned by reading them was spread

abroad, I was invited to several places to read them, at a considerable distance; and by this means the concern was propagated.

"About this time, our absenting ourselves from church, contrary, as was alleged, to the laws of the land, was taken notice of; and we were called upon by the court, to assign our reasons for it, and to declare what denomination we were of. As we knew but little of any denomination of dissenters, except Quakers, we were at a loss what name to assume. At length, recollecting that Luther was a noted reformer, and that his doctrines were agreeable to our sentiments, and had been of special service to us, we declared ourselves Lutherans; and thus we continued till Providence afforded us an unexpected opportunity of hearing the Rev. Mr. William Robinson."

Here, Sir, it may be proper for me to lay aside the person of my informer for a while, and interrupt the connexion of his relation, to give you some account of the travels and successes of that zealous, faithful and laborious minister of Christ, the late Mr. Robinson, whose dear memory will mingle with my softest and most grateful thoughts, as long as I am capable of reflection. He was in the ministry about six years, and never took the charge of a congregation till a few months before his happy and triumphant exit. The necessitous circumstances of many vacancies; and the prospects of more extensive usefulness, engaged him to expose his shattered constitution to all the hardships and fatigues of almost uninterrupted itinerations; and it has been my lot to trace his travels in sundry parts of Pennsylvania, Maryland and Virginia; and I cannot recollect one place in which he had officiated for any time, where there were not some illustrious effects of his ministry. He had a noble, disinterested ambition to preach the gospel where Christ was not named; and therefore, by the permission of the Presbytery, he took a journey through the new settlements in Pennsylvania, Virginia and North Carolina, in which he continued about two years, oppressed with the usual difficulties a weakly constitution finds in travelling a wilderness, and animated only by his glorious successes. He continued for some time in Lunenburg, a county

about one hundred miles southwest of this, where, (as I shall
have occasion to observe more fully hereafter,) a small number
of Presbyterians from the northern colonies were settled, inter-
mixed with a number of loose Virginians; and there he was the
happy instrument of reclaiming many thoughtless creatures, and
founding a flourishing congregation. In Amelia also, a county
somewhat nearer this than the former, his labors were extensively blessed; and while he was there, or near it, some of the
people in Hanover, having had some imperfect information of
him, sent him an invitation to come and preach to them, though
they knew very little of his character or method of preaching,
only that it was uncommon, and tended to awaken people.
They ventured to make an appointment for him to preach at
their reading house (if I may so call it) before they received
any promise from him by their messenger; and with much difficulty he came against the day appointed. Some of the people
were anxious to discover his principles privately, in the morning,
before he was to preach; but knew not how, till they fell upon
the device of asking his opinion of some books they approved
of. Upon his declaring his approbation of these tests of orthodoxy, they were transported with the most pleasing expectations, and with eager impatience, attended him to the place
where he was to preach.

I shall now reassume the person of my informer, and proceed
in his narrative, "On the sixth of July, 1743, Mr. Robinson
preached his first sermon to us, from Luke 13: 3, and continued
with us preaching four days successively. The congregation
was large the first day; and as the report of him spread, it vastly
increased on the three ensuing. It is hard for the liveliest imagination to form an image of the condition of the assembly on
these glorious days of the Son of man. Such of us as had been
hungering for the word before, were lost in an agreeable confusion of various passions, surprised, astonished, pleased, enrap-
tured! so that we were hardly capable of self-government; and
some could not refrain from publicly declaring their transport.
We were overwhelmed with the thoughts of the unexpected

goodness of God, in allowing us to hear the gospel preached in a manner that surpassed even our former wishes, and much more our hopes. Many that came through curiosity, were pricked to the heart; and but few in the numerous assemblies on these four days appeared unaffected. They returned astonished, alarmed with apprehensions of their dangerous condition, convinced of their former entire ignorance of religion, and anxiously inquiring, what they should do to be saved. And there is reason to believe there was as much good done by these four sermons, as by all the sermons preached in these parts before or since.

"Before Mr. Robinson left us, he successfully endeavoured to correct some of our Antinomian mistakes, and to bring us to carry on the worship of God more regularly at our meetings. He advised us to meet to read good sermons, and to begin and conclude with prayer and singing of Psalms, which till then we had omitted. When we next met, we complied with his directions; and when all the rest refused, I read and prayed with trembling and diffidence; which method was observed in sundry places, till we were furnished with a minister. The blessing of God remarkably attended these more private means; and it was really astonishing to observe the solemn impressions begun or continued in many, by hearing good discourses read. I had repeated invitations to come to many places round, some of them thirty or forty miles distant, to read; with which I generally complied. Considerable numbers were wont to attend, with eager attention and awful solemnity; and sundry were, in a judgment of charity, thoroughly turned to God, and thereupon erected meetinghouses, and chose readers among themselves, by which the work was more extensively carried on.

"Soon after our father, Mr. Robinson, left us, the Rev. Mr. John Blair paid us a short visit; and truly, he came to us in the fulness of the gospel of Christ. Former impressions were ripened, and new formed on many hearts. One night, in particular, a whole house full of people was quite overcome with the power of the word, particularly of one pungent sentence that dropped from his lips; and they could hardly sit or stand, or keep their passions under any proper restraints, so general was the concern during his stay with us; and so ignorant were we of the danger persons in such a case were in of apostasy, which unhappy observation has since taught us, that we pleased ourselves with the expectation of the gathering of more people to the divine Shiloh, than now seem to have been actually gathered to him; though there be still the greatest reason to hope, that sundry bound themselves to the Lord in an everlasting covenant, never to be forgotten.

"Some time after this, the Rev. Mr. John Roan was sent by the Presbytery of Newcastle (under whose immediate care we had voluntarily placed ourselves) to supply us. He continued with us longer than either of the former; and the happy effects of his ministrations are still apparent, in many instances. He preached at sundry places at the earnest solicitations of the people, which was the happy occasion of beginning and promoting the religious concern, where there were little appearances of it before. This, together with his speaking pretty freely about the degeneracy of the clergy in this colony, gave a general alarm, and some measures were concerted to suppress us. To incense the indignation of the government the more, a perfidious wretch deposed, he heard Mr. Roan use some blasphemous expressions in his sermon, and speak in the most shocking and reproachful manner of the established church. An indictment was thereupon drawn up against Mr. Roan, (though by that time he had departed the colony,) and some of the people who had invited him to preach at their houses, were cited to appear before the General Court, (which, in this government, consists of the Governor or Commander-in-chief, and His Majesty's council,) and two of them were fined twenty shillings sterling, besides the costs, which in one of the cases would have amounted to near fifty pounds, had the evidences demanded their due. While my cause was upon trial, I had reason to rejoice that the throne of grace is accessible in all places, and that helpless creatures can waft up their desires unseen, to God, in the midst of a crowd. Six evidences were cited to prove the indictment against Mr.

Roan; but their depositions were in his favor; and as for the evidence mentioned just now, who accused him of blasphemy against God and the church, when he heard of Messrs. G. Tennent's and S. Finley's arrival, he fled, and has not returned since; so that the indictment was dropped. I had reason to fear being banished the colony; and all circumstances seemed to threaten the extirpation of religion among the dissenters in these parts.

"In these difficulties we lay, without any person of a public character to appear in our favor; whereupon we determined to acquaint the Synod of New York with our case; hoping that a synodical representation of it to our worthy Governor, the Hon. Sir William Gooch, might free him from the misinformations under which he labored, and procure us the liberties granted to Protestant Dissenters by the Act of Toleration. Accordingly, four of us went to the Synod, May, 1745, when the Lord favored us with success. The Synod, being informed of our difficulties, and presuming they might be removed by an impartial representation of our affairs, drew up an address to our Governor, and sent the Rev. Messrs. G. Tennent and Samuel Finley to wait on his honor to present it, and to officiate a few days among us. Sir William received them with condescension and respect, and granted them liberty to preach in Hanover. By this means, the tremendous cloud that hung over us was dissipated for a time, and our languid hopes were revived. Mr. Tennent and Mr. Finley continued with us about a week; and though the deluge of passion in which we were at first overwhelmed, was by this time somewhat abated, yet much good was done by their ministry. The people of God were refreshed, and sundry careless sinners were awakened. Some that had confided before in their moral conduct and religious duties, were convinced of the depravity of their nature, and the necessity of being renewed in the spirit of their mind; though indeed there were but few unregenerate persons among us at that time, that could claim so regular a character; the generality of professors indulging themselves in criminal liberties, and being remiss in the duties of religion; which alas! is too commonly the case still in such parts of the colony as the late revival did not extend to.

"After these gentlemen had left us, we continued vacant for a considerable time, and kept up our meetings for reading and prayer in sundry places; and the Lord favored us at these occasions with his gracious presence. I was again repeatedly presented and fined in court for absenting myself from church, and keeping up unlawful meetings, as they were called; but the bush flourished in the flames.

"The next that were appointed to supply us, were the Rev. Messrs. William Tennent and Samuel Blair. They waited on the Governor, and readily obtained his permission to officiate among us. Their labors were not in vain in the Lord. They administered the sacrament of the Lord's Supper among us before their departure; which was the first administration of that heavenly ordinance among us since our dissent from the Church of England; and we have reason to remember it till our last moments, as a most glorious day of the Son of man. The assembly was large, and the novelty of the mode of administration did peculiarly engage their attention. The children were abundantly fed, and others were brought to hunger and thirst after righteousness. It appeared as one of the days of heaven to some of us; and we could hardly help wishing we could, with Joshua, have delayed the revolutions of the heavens, to prolong it.

"Messrs. Tennent and Blair continued with us about a fortnight; and immediately after their departure, Mr. Whitefield came and preached four or five days in these parts; which was the happy means of giving us further encouragement, and engaging others to the Lord, especially among the Church people, who received his doctrines more readily than they would from ministers of the Presbyterian denomination.

"After his departure, we were destitute of a minister, and followed our usual method of reading and prayer at our meetings, till the Rev. Mr. Davies, our present pastor, was sent by the Presbytery to supply us about six weeks, in spring, Anno 1747, when our discouragements from the government were renewed and multiplied: for on one Sunday, the Governor's proclamation was set up at our meetinghouse, strictly requiring all magistrates to suppress and prohibit, as far as they lawfully could, all itinerant preachers, &c., which occasioned us to forebear reading that day, till we had time to deliberate and consult what was expedient to do; but how joyfully were we surprised before the next Sabbath, when we unexpectedly heard that Mr. Davies was come to preach so long among us; and especially, that he had qualified himself according to law, and obtained the licensure of four meetinghouses among us, which had never been done before! Thus, when our hopes were expiring, and our liberties more precarious than ever, we were suddenly advanced to a more secure situation. Man's extremity is the Lord's opportunity. For this seasonable instance of the interposition of divine providence, we desire to offer our grateful praises; and we importune the friends of Zion generously to concur in the delightful employ."

The term "Great Awakening" should probably be confined to the great outpouring of religious enthusiasm which in the 1740's followed George Whitefield's first preaching tour. However, the waves of evangelical pietism and revival sentiment thus unleashed rolled on right through the eighteenth century. As new territory was settled, it was visited by itinerant pietist missionaries. By the end of the century, revivalism had made its way to the northern reaches of British settlement, in provinces which had remained loyal to the King during the American Revolution. The following account by the New Brunswick and Nova Scotia Baptist, Joseph Crandall, illustrates this expansion.

JOSEPH CRANDALL

New Brunswick Baptist History.
Manuscript in Maritime Baptist Historical Collection,
Acadia University, Wolfville, Nova Scotia

I was born in a place called Tivertown in Rhode Island. My parents Webber Crandall and Mercy Vaughan, emigrated from that country to Nova Scotia about one year before the revolution. The country was extremely poor, and but thinly settled.

The inhabitants were poor and there were no schools there at that time. When I was ten or twelve years of age I was sent from home. The woman with whom I lived taught me to spell a little. Afterwards I attended an evening school for about three months. I think the Holy Spirit moved on my mind when I was quite a young lad. One Sabbath morning, my mother called us all in and reproved us for being at play on the Lords day; she read the Bible and wept and, although I cannot remember all she said, some of her words and her solemn looks were never erased from my mind. When about thirteen years of age I was called to the death bed of my mother. I was much alarmed to see my beloved mother so pale and deathlike. She said to me, "that she had sent for me to hear her last farewell." She said "she was going to leave us all and go to her Saviour where she would be happy." After some time she looked earnestly at me and said "Joseph, the Lord has a great work for you to do, when I am dead and gone." I believe my dear mother was under the influence of the Holy Spirit, and is now with her precious Saviour in Heaven.

I recollect one day a couple of strangers came to the house where I was living. They talked of a strange man that was preaching in Windsor and adjoining places; he preached in the night, and people were becoming crazy and talked about their souls. My father had heard this man preach and as he happened to be there at the time he explained to the strangers that this preacher Henry Allin was a "New Light" and that the "New Light" were the people of God for they were Christians and that none could go to Heaven unless they were converted.

Some time after this Mr. John Sargent came to Chester, he was called a "New Light" preacher; then came Handly Chipman and Harris Harding. Their arrival was followed by a great excitement among the people, quite a number professed to be converted, among the number being the Vaughans, the Floyds, and many other families followed the new preacher. Some young people about my own age professed to be converted, and although I attended all the meetings and fully believed it was the Lords work, yet my heart was hard and unmoved and I thought at the time that the Lord had left me to perish in my sins, and justly too, for I was one of the greatest sinners on earth. From that time I became more hardened in sin and was often in despair, sometimes I wished I had never been born. My parents were now both dead and I was left a poor orphan boy in an unfriendly world. For five years I continued wandering down the broad road to ruin; with heedless feet I madly trod the path to endless woe, and would have sunk in firey flames, but mercy interposed. In the midst of all my sinful career I always had a tender conscience. Two kinds of evil I detested, viz. drunkenness and thieving. And Oh! how thankful I ought to be to the Lord who kept me back from even these heinous sins.

The people with whom I lived told me that I had no soul, because I was not sprinkled in my infancy. I thought I ought to be like other people, so I went to a venerable old Presbyterian minister and he kindly performed the unscriptural act for me. I must have been nearly fourteen years of age when this took place, and I came home from the meeting house supposing I had done some wonderful deed (This affair took place before the new ministers and reformation previously mentioned came). Otherwise I would have better understood my duty.

Some time after this I left Chester and went to Liverpool N.S. where I remained two years — was employed at this place in Cod fishing. My life in Liverpool was exceedingly sinful — From Liverpool I returned to Chester, from there I went to Falmouth and then to Newport — was engaged for a time in freighting lumber from Shubenacadie to Windsor. About this time there was to be a meeting of the Christians from different parts of the country. David Vaughan had promised that the schooner in which I sailed should carry the pilgrims to Onslow. After some hesitation I consented that they should be carried with us, but my cousin John Vaughan refused to go. We left Newport on Friday and reached Onslow on Sabbath morning. The next week I collected a number of young men and went down the bay to have a regular pleasure sail. We returned on

Saturday and Sabbath morning I went to the meeting which was held at the house of Mr. Philip Higgins. I cannot say that I had any great anxiety about the meetings, except my desire to see Harris Harding who was high in my esteem since the time of the reformation at Chester. When I entered the house the meeting had commenced — I have no knowledge of anything that was said by any person in the meeting. The moment I entered the house, the glorious majesty of the Divine Being appeared to open before the eyes of my understanding (I beheld no object with my bodily eyes) and I saw myself justly condemned to endless misery. I saw no way of escape until suddenly a glorious light shone from the excellent Majesty and I saw the way of Salvation was Gods work and not mine. I felt as I had never felt before, although amongst strangers, I could not hold my peace. My hard heart was at last broken, and I had such a view of a perishing world lying in ruin as I never could express. To the great surprise of all present I began to speak and try to tell what I felt and saw. My mind was completely absorbed in the solemn and marvellous scene. It appeared to me that the whole human race lay in open ruin and were altogether at the disposal of that Holy Being whose bright glory had so overwhelmed my soul. I saw mercy so connected with the justice of God, that they were both one, that what God had done in the person of Christ was alone sufficient to save all that came to God for mercy through Jesus Christ. I felt that the whole world ought to know what I felt and saw, for indeed it appeared of more importance to me than the whole world. I continued speaking (as the people told me afterwards) for more than an hour, for I could not hold my peace, for it was a stream of living water flowing into my soul and then bursting forth like a stream from an overflowing fountain. The work of sinners lay before me, like a broad field to which I could see no end. . . .

CHAPTER 3   Results and
                                             Significance

The total impact which the Great Awakening had on colonial America is difficult to measure. Statistical computations of
the number of converts are difficult to establish: records are
lacking; many converted suddenly in the revival might well
have ultimately done so and others quickly backslid; the backcountry had its own rules. Certainly, in intellectual terms the
revival completely destroyed any religio-ideological consensus
which may have existed in colonial America, produced a
dynamic new spiritual posture in evangelical pietism, and re-
aligned existing denominations while fragmenting others. Colonial America was always a crazy-quilt of religious sects, but the
revival ensured that denominational fragmentation dominated
by strong overtones of Protestant pietism would prevail in
what would become the United States and Canada. The absence of a dominant religious denomination doomed the con-
cept of a church establishment, and pietism came to stress not
simply disestablishment, but the "high wall of Separation" between church and state. The Awakening is also credited with
giving an impetus to the founding of new American universities
by denominations such as the Presbyterians and the Baptists
which greatly profited from revival.

More difficult to establish than formal intellectual impact was
the effect of the Awakening on public morality and popular

patterns of thinking. Proponents always claimed moral reformation as one of the boons of revival, but certainly not all observers of the colonial scene agreed that there was a reduction of sinfulness on the part of the populace. Whether evangelical pietism, which became without doubt an important component of the colonial ethos — at least for large segments of the population — was more important in directing potential secular discontent into other-worldly channels or in radicalizing the population by calling into question and undermining secular authority in church and state has long been a moot point. Certainly both features were inherent in the movement.

Finally, there is the matter of cooperation among various denominations and sects which shared a pietistic viewpoint. Attempts to see a new ecumenical spirit in the Awakening among both proponents and opponents of the revival must confront the indisputable fact that pietism produced a good deal of fragmentation and dissension. Moreover, cooperation even among sympathetic evangelicals had clear limitations.

Despite all the qualifications, there can be no doubt that the American colonies were somehow significantly different after the Great Awakening than they had been before. The nature and extent of the changes remain subjects of great debate.

One of the principal results of the Great Awakening was to destroy permanently any ideational consensus which may have existed in American Puritanism. While Puritanism had never been a single doctrine, its various wings were never so clearly recognizable or divided before 1740 as they became afterward. Puritans came to disagree publicly over a variety of critical issues, none more significant than the question of the qualifications for admission to the Lord's Supper, which raised the whole problem of church membership. Who was eligible for membership in the churches and how was this eligibility to be tested? From a great spectrum of answers, at least four positions emerged. That represented by John Cotton in the following selection was probably a majority one in the years immediately preceding and following the Awakening. It involved support for the halfway covenant (by which children of those baptized within the church but not themselves eligible for communion were baptized) and a distinction between these "halfway" members and those members in "full communion." Cotton was an active "New Light" in the 1740's.

JOHN COTTON

The General Practice of the Churches of New-England, Relating to Baptism, Vindicated: Or, Some Essays on this Important Question, Whether the Practice of Persons Owning or Renewing the Covenant, and Having Baptism for their Children Without Coming into Full Communion, Be Warrantable?

Boston, 1772, 1–10

QUEST.

WHETHER the practice of persons owning or renewing the covenant, and having baptism for their children, without coming immediately to full communion, be warrantable?

Arguments for the affirmative.

I. I THINK the famous Mr. *Mitchell's* argument unanswerable. 1st. The whole visible church under the new testament is to be baptized. 2d. If a man be once in the church (whether admitted at age or in infancy) nothing less than censurable evil can put him out. 3d. If the parent be in the visible church, his infant child is also."

This was the chief argument that convinced Dr. *Increase Mather.* It is impossible to get over this argument, but by saying, that not coming immediately to the LORD's table is a *censurable* evil, a sin that deserves excommunication. But did any church ever hold this? Who has heard or read of any person's being laid under the church-censure meerly on this account? I grant, that the *contempt* of this ordinance deserves excommunication, but not the meer abstaining from it for a while. That may proceed from too high thoughts of the ordinance, and low thoughts of themselves. To cut off such would be *a breaking the bruised reed* with a witness, as Mr. *Leonard* justly observes in the church records. We would bear with a communicant for not coming to the LORD's table if he declares it is from the scruples of conscience respecting his state, and not from contempt of the ordinance: Much more should we bear with a member, that never communicated. Such should be dealt with in *the ministry of the word and from the pulpit,* and not by church censure. They should not be treated as *delinquent members* (as in the case of *heresy* or *scandal*) but be used with all tenderness.

II. All the arguments brought for infant baptism in general do prove that baptism ought to be administered in the latitude pleaded for. These arguments all center in this, *that if the parents be in the covenant, the children are so likewise, and so ought to have the seal of the covenant.* Now it is granted on all hands, that the parents in question are in the covenant, consequently then children are so too; why then should they not be baptized? To deny the validity of this way of arguing is to give up the cause entirely to the *Anabaptists*; and there is no way left to confute them, and their demand is just when they call for a direct scripture for infant baptism; as some demand a direct scripture in this case, which is exactly to tread in their steps. In short, there is as much proof for this point, as for infant baptism; we argue by *scripture consequence* both in the one case and the same consequences prove both points.

III. CHRIST says, Luke xviii. 16. *Suffer little children to come unto me, and forbid them not; for of such is the kingdom of* GOD, *i. e.* Such are of my church. (This is the ground of the rebuke.) The same may be said of the children in question. They are the children of members, therefore members. And here we may observe, That CHRIST was never so angry with his good disciples upon any occasion, as for this debarring of the subjects of his kingdom being brought to him. Let us fear lest he be as angry with us, if we do the same. The disciples thought that they were not good men that brought these children; they exhibited no precise evidence of grace to their view; neither does CHRIST so much as intimate that they were gracious. But the ground he seems to go upon was, that as they were members of the church, they had a right to bring their children;

thereby letting us know, that it is *visible membership* gives the right. If you say, their bringing their children was evidence enough of their faith in CHRIST, the same I say of the persons in question. If you say further, CHRIST would never have commended them for bringing their children, if they had not been real disciples. I answer, this is plainly begging the question, and it renders CHRIST'S answer to the disciples improper, which should have been (according to their notion) an express declaration of the *parent's fitness*, and not of the *children's interest in the covenant* or visible membership.

IV. "When a man according to scripture rule is become a member of the visible church, and there is no rule in the word to cast him out of the church, such a person has a right to have his children baptized."

V. If these persons are subject to the *rod* or to church-government, they are intitled to the *privileges* of CHRIST'S kingdom. We ought not to separate what God has joined together. And we have no business to *judge them that are without*, as we really do if they are entitled to no privileges at all.

VI. Those that submit to CHRIST'S *discipline* cannot with any colour of reason be excluded from *discipleship*. And if disciples, they have a right to baptism for their children. And here I would mention that famous text so much alledged by *Anabaptists* and their opponents, *Matt.* xxviii. 20. *Go disciple*[1] *all nations, baptizing them*, &c. Here infants (as part of *nations*)are to be *discipled* and *baptized*. And if *discipled*, all the privileges of disciples belong to them; and when demanded (after they are grown up) cannot justly be withheld from them, without they put a bar in their own way by their wickedness.[2]

VII. If you exclude baptized persons (of regular lives) from bringing their children to baptism, you treat them as *Pagans*

---

[1] So the word runs in the original Greek.

[2] Their *discipleship* is also proved from several other texts by all the writers for infant baptism. To be *discipled* is to be admitted into CHRIST'S school and family in order to be taught when capable, &c.

and infidels; you practically say, they have no part in the LORD;
you in effect excommunicate them and shut them all out of
heaven; for there is no salvation out of the church: You make
them visible members of Satan's kingdom; for there is no medium here, a man must be of the one or the other.

VIII. CHRIST says, *feed my lambs*; but this, instead of feeding
them, is a thrusting them out of the fold: Instead of *carrying
them in our arms* we cut off their heads. And how dreadful is
the thought!

IX. If this rigid principle should prevail, in a few years (according to human prospect) nine tenths of the inhabitants will
be in the condition of *Pagans* and *Infidels*; and even the name
of Christianity will be in danger of being lost among this
people.[3]

But this would be better (some say) than *to come with a lie
in their mouths.* I answer, they do not come with a lie in their
mouths, if they act conscientiously in what they do, if they
come out of a sense of the command, and if (as far as they
know their own hearts) they are sincere in what they profess,
though they cannot say it is a *gracious sincerity.* It is the *wilful
hypocrite* that lies to GOD and perjures himself, who (conscious of his insincerity) does all to be seen of men, &c. I am
persuaded and it may be easily proved from the word of GOD,
that the former sort do not offend GOD so much by coming in
this manner though they have no real grace, as they would do
by wholly neglecting the duty. The total neglect is worse than

---

[3] "It is to me a confirmation to observe *de facto* (says Mr. *Mitchell*)
that in the way of *successive baptizing* the children of all that had a
standing in the *visible church* (though with too much *laxness* and *corrup-
tion* for want of *discipline*) the LORD hath continued *religion* among
christian people from age to age: Whereas the like continuance and
preservation of true religion could not have been hoped for, nor probable in the contrary way. It was never heard of in the world from
Abraham to this day (since GOD appointed an *entring sign*, or such a
livery to be worn by his people to distinguish them from the world;)
that a people did continue for any length of time to be religious, who
were either all, or the greater part of them *uncircumcised* or *unbaptised.*
The laying aside of *circumcision* among the *Midianites*, (for they did by

the undue performance. And the same may be said of every duty.

This makes way for the considering some other objections.

I. It is objected, but these persons do not come immediately to the LORD's supper; and therefore they ought to be shut out from other privileges until they will partake of the whole. I answer,

1st. The church in all ages has been larger in admitting to baptism, than the LORD's supper. In the primitive church there were three sorts. 1st. *Catechumeni* or well disposed *Heathens* under instruction. 2d. *Initiati* or baptized persons. 3d. *Confirmati*, confirmed members. They used to wait some time to see how persons behaved after they were baptized, before they admitted them to the holy mysteries. And I might prove the point from the practice of all churches since; but it would take up too long a time.

2d. I would mention some maxims or principles of famous divines, which carry their own weight with them. As 1st. Baptism belongs to the disciples as such; the LORD's supper to *self-examining* disciples. 2d. Baptism is a sacrament of initiation or entrance into the church; the other of confirmation or growth in grace. 3d. Membership in the universal church gives a right to baptism; but membership in a particular church to the LORD's supper. Those that the Apostles baptized as it were at large, must be joined to a particular church before they could receive the LORD's supper. 4th. Covenant interest alone giveth right to baptism, but not to the LORD's supper. It is a

---

times lay it aside, may be plainly gathered from *Exod.* iv. 24, 26.) was quickly followed with the utter loss of all true religion among them, and other of the posterity of *Abraham* and *Keturah.* I know the bare having of baptism does not always keep true religion; but sure it is, that the *want of it* will quickly lose religion among a people. To say that a people may be religious well enough without baptism, would be to reflect upon the wisdom of CHRIST, in appointing such an *external sign* of *Christianity*, which surely was no needless thing. It is easy to see that in the way yourself and some others go, *the bigger half of the people in this country will in a little time be unbaptised.*"

Letter to *Inc. Mather*, p. 4. 5.

great mistake to think, that the parents *immediate fitness* for the LORD's supper is the ground of baptizing their children; but it is the parents and so the childrens being in the covenant. We often have reason to think that some communicants are *unfit* for the LORD's supper; but we cannot exclude them from that ordinance or from baptism for their children, being neither heretical or scandalous. The reason is, because they are under the covenant. The same may be said in the other case. 5th. *That uncleanness* would debar from coming to the passover, which did not unfit for the other ordinance of circumcision. These several particulars import, that we should not be altogether so *strict* in admission to baptism, as to the LORD's supper.

3d. I answer, "A mans not joining to a particular church may be owing to the *weakness of his tender conscience,* which scrupleth his fitness for the LORD's supper; and yet would gladly have himself and his consecrated to the LORD, yea and rejoice to be under the government and laws of CHRIST in particular churches."

4th. If the knowledge of a man's good estate (as they hold) is a necessary qualification for the LORD's supper, it is his duty to stay away until he has this knowledge; and yet not neglect other duties in the mean time.

5th. If such persons are real and hearty in renewing covenant they will soon come further; if they are not, they had better remain where they are. It will be more for the honour of the church; for how often do those who are only under a common work of the spirit, lose their convictions, and (by their apostacy) become a scandal to religion and to the church that admits them? And hence we may see the impropriety of vehemently urging persons to come immediately into full communion, when they do not find a *freedom* in themselves to do it.

6th. We ought rather to encourage persons to come as far as they see light in the path of duty, than to lay discouragements and stumbling-blocks in their way. This is truly to *carry the lambs in our arms.*

II. It is objected, But if all baptized persons are members already, why should they own the covenant? Is it not that, that makes them members? I answer, no: A person doth not become any more a member than he was before by renewing the covenant. It is only a recognition or taking possession of his right in the manner the church thinks proper. It is like an officer's taking an oath for the faithful discharge of his office: It is not the oath that constitutes the officer, but the *commission* which he had before. There is no impropriety in calling all baptized persons *compleat members* as our ancient Divines and the Synod *expressly* do. Membership is a thing that cannot be increased or diminished; there is no *magis* or *minus* (more or less) here: A man is a member or no member; there is no medium: But their CAPACITIES of ACTING are not the same; they may be widely different. An infant or a communicant (become *non-compos*) cannot receive the LORD's supper; yet they are compleat members. And there is no such a thing as *halfmembership* or *half-covenanting*, and it is injurious to use such an expression. But what advantage is it to renew covenant then? I answer, This is a *meer prudential* of the church, to make the more *deep* and more *durable* impressions on the persons concerned; to give them proper ideas of the solemnity of the affair; and also to impress on others a solemn sense of their covenant engagements, by a repetition of the covenant in their hearing. They have the same end in it that whole churches have, when they renew covenant *openly* and *explicitly*, as the churches were wont to do formerly, and this church more than once in my Grandfather's days. But it never entered into their hearts, that they made any *addition* to their membership by it. So it is in the present case. I am sorry to see that this custom of renewing covenant is so misunderstood by many; they seem to have got a notion, that by renewing covenant they are made members. But this is a mistake; they are no more members than they were before: And the practice had better laid aside, than to be thus abused by such gross apprehensions.

III. But it is further objected, it is only *grace* that gives a right to either seal; and therefore a person ought not to come until he knows his grace. I answer,

1st. This objection doth not reach the case of those that were baptized in infancy; but those only that come for baptism at adult age. The former are members already, and therefore if we go to *purge* the church of them, or refuse to let them renew covenant, (which is the same thing) let them ever be so blameless in their walk, we must go further still, and purge the communicants likewise (who renew covenant every time they come to the sacrament) and turn out all that we think have not grace, or that dare not say they are converted. And where we must stop no man can say. In short, this is running directly into the most rigid principles of the *Separates,* who are for purging the church. We have no more warrant to cast baptized persons out of the church than communicants: And if we do the one we must do the other also, when there is the same ground for it, that is, reason to fear they are graceless. Indeed if *heresy* or *scandal* can be proved upon either sort, let them be cast out in God's name; but not otherwise.

2d. These Persons in question exhibit those *signs of grace* which our opponents set up as the *only standard* for the church to judge by. They explode an account or *relation* of experiences, at least think them unnecessary; and make profession and practice the only criterion of judgment. Thus Mr. *Green,* one of the *Connecticut* champions for the new scheme; he says in his late treatise, p. 57–8 "In the admission of persons, we are not to judge from the account of *inward experiences:* This is not laid down in scripture as the rule of publick judgment, but profession and practice." To this we entirely agree with respect to *baptism.* Why then will they not suffer persons of *regular practice* to renew the covenant, when they desire it? or in other words, to add profession to their practice, which (according to them, is all that is necessary; and so to have baptism for their children? this would put an end to the controversy.

Here, by the way, I cannot help observing, how ridiculous it is to insist that none but *gracious persons* ought to partake of the seals; and yet at the same time to say, that it is unnecessary to give an account of the *actings of grace in their souls,* which is what we call experiences. This seems to me to be a direct contradiction. Such an account is really *essential* to their scheme; and if separated from it, it falls to the ground; and they really (after all their noise about grace) take up with lesser evidences than we do in regard of the LORD's supper.

3d. If this doctrine be true, then it will follow, that no believer while in the dark ought to come to either ordinance, or even present his child to baptism; for then he implicitly renews covenant; which must not be done in a state of darkness. And what confusion would this bring into the church? We should have but thin communions, if the members every time they come must know they have grace.

4th. According to this scheme, no person ought to engage in any duty whatsoever, until he knows he has grace; For he is in danger of *lying to* GOD, or dealing *falsely* in the discharge of it; which is the grand objection in the present case.

5th. According to this scheme, *Hezekiah* and *Josiah* were to blame, for bringing their people in general to renew covenant, when they had reason to fear the greater part of them would come with *a lye* in their mouths, and they had better have let it alone.

6th. I have observed before; if persons know not that they have grace, yet are conscious of their sincerity in what they do, they had better come than stay away. And if they should be really destitute of grace, their coming will be less offensive to GOD than the omission would be. Reformation and renewings of covenant when only proceeding from a common work of GOD's spirit, have been a means of removing or preventing judgments, as is evident from many places of scripture.

And here I would mention one thing; I should be glad to hear as much of the danger of the *total omission* of these duties, as of the performing them in a *wrong manner.* The *Jew* that did not circumcise his child was to be *cut off from* GOD's *people, i. e.*

put to death: But no such severe judgment was threatned against the unregenerate person, that circumcised his child. And *Moses* himself had like to have lost his life, for the omission of this duty.

7th. *John* the Baptist and CHRIST's disciples did not ask those they baptized, whether they knew they had grace. But upon *their confession of their sins* and promising reformation, they immediately baptized them, *Matt.* 3, 6.

8th. If this church should agree to renew covenant at this day openly and explicitly as churches did formerly for the strengthening their covenant engagements, it would be proper and necessary to call upon all the children of the church to join with us in it, as our Fathers did, as we may find on our church-records. And who in this case would dare to forbid or exclude them, though they did not come immediately to the LORD's table? And if not why should they be excluded when they come *one by one?*

9th. If the knowledge of our good estate be necessary in order to partaking of the seals, it must amount to a *certain* knowledge. For how can a *meer hope* entitle us to it? How know we but it is the hope of the hypocrite? Suppose a king should give such and such privileges to persons so and so qualified, it will not do for persons to come and say they *hope* they have those qualifications; they must *certainly* make out to their own and others satisfaction that they have them, or they have no business to put in their claim. So that this doctrine is come to this at last, that nothing but *full assurance* will warrant our coming either to baptism or the LORD's supper. And if we have this before we come, what need we come at all? At least we need not come for this end, to get our evidences and comforts strengthened; they being already come to their full strength.

IVth objection. But why do you exclude any baptized person at all from bringing their children to baptism, if they are all members? I answer, the reason is, because of their vicious lives. If a person be a lyar, swearer, sabbath-breaker, whoremonger, &c. he ought to be dealt with, and if he remain impenitent to be cut off. In this case he forfeits his privilege. And this is the reason why persons are propounded, that if any know they are guilty of such things, they may object and get them excluded.

Vth and last objection. This will bring in impurity into the church. I answer, Diligent attendance to discipline, and not *curtailing the covenant* will keep the churches pure. The contrary doctrine rather tends to impurity: For persons, if debarred from renewing covenant and bringing their children, will be tempted from their great fondness for their offspring, to come too rashly to the LORD's table. And the church will likewise be tempted to be *lax* in their admissions, to prevent the complaints of such persons, and to remove the reproach that such swarms of children among them are in a state of *heathenism.*

Several other weighty considerations might have been mentioned, but I forbear. I shall finish with observing, That this was the principle of almost all the first Fathers in the country; my Great-grandfather *Cotton,* Mr. *Norton,* the famous Mr. *Shepard,* Mess'rs *Wilson, Mather, Allen, Rogers,* and many others. And the practice was recommended by a *Synod* of all the churches of the *Massachusetts* Colony in the year 1662. And it was agreeable to the sentiments of my Grandfather *Cotton* the former Minister of this church, as I find by a manuscript written by his own hand. And it has been practised by the generality of the churches for more than an hundred years past.

One alternative to prevailing Puritan practices was that offered by Jonathan Edwards. Since the days of Solomon Stoddard, Edwards' Northampton church had employed the common alternative to the halfway covenant: an admission to membership of all those who made a "profession of faith" intellectually assenting to the doctrines of Christianity and the church. Edwards attempted to alter this practice and thus provoked a dispute which ultimately cost him his job. The best short statement of the Edwardsean position is probably the following letter written by Edwards to the Reverend Peter Clark, a minister Edwards feared might attack him in the public prints.

An Unpublished Letter by Jonathan Edwards, *George Peirce Clark,* ed., *The New England Quarterly, XXIX, 1956, pp. 228–233.*

Northampton May 7. 1750.

REV. & HONOURED SIR.

There having been Application made to you from Time to Time by my People, in an Affair that most nearly concerns me occasiond (I suppose) by Intimations They have received from some of the neighbouring ministers of what they knew of your abilities, and something They had hear'd you had said particularly relating to this affair; and there having been an Intercourse by Letters between you and my People, and also the neighbouring ministers about this matter; I thought it not amiss for me also to write to you, & say something for my self. I don't know what has been said to you by Those who have applied to you, nor what Representations They have made of my Principles & Conduct: But I know some of Them have been greatly engaged in opposition to me in this affair, and have been apt to view Things which I say & do in a most disadvantageous Light; and therefore I have Reason to expect they [will] make an answerable Representation of Them to others. I know by your Letters, which I have seen, you have had some great misrepresentations made to you; and know not how far your mind may be prepossessed with such prejudices as mankind in general are very liable to in cases of controversy, by receiving accounts from Time to Time, from such [only] as [?] rise [?] on one side only. But nevertheless am encouraged to write on my own behalf, from the Esteem I have long entertain'd of your Judgment, from some of your writings, particularly your defence of Infant Baptism against my Class-mate Walton, and also by the appearances I saw of Candour in your Late Letters to Maj. Pomroy & Mr. Billing. and my writ-

ing appear'd to me the more requisite from what you signify in your Letter to Maj. Pomroy of your Thoughts of
writing & sending to my People your Opinion of my Book
lately publish'd, after you should have had opportunity to
read it. — I have taken a great deal of Pains to explain my
self both in what I have written & spoken; But yet I am so
unhappy as to be misunderstood by many. notwithstanding all I can say for my self, there appears (as seems to
me) a strange disposition to take me wrong, and to entertain uncharitable and injurious Thoughts of my meaning,
& also concerning the Principles & dispositions I act from,
and the Ends They suppose I secretly aim at. By which
means many at a distance have conceived very disadvantageous & injurious notions of me. — I am far from pretending to a discriminating Judgment of men's spiritual
state, so as infallibly to determine who are true converts
& who are not, or imagining that I, or any Body else is
sufficient for the Execution of any such design as the setting up a Pure Church consisting only of true Converts.
Nor do I claim any Power above my Neighbours in this
Respect. I have seen enough of my own fallibleness, & of
the uncertainty of my [own] Judgment in things of this
nature, I think, forever to guard me from such folly, or to
assume to my self the divine Prerogative in this Respect.
I have constantly born a full Testimony in Preaching,
writing & conversation against the assuming & arrogance
of such as set up Themselves to be discerners of mens
Hearts, and have promoted separation, under a notion of
setting up pure Churches. I have ever been an Enemy to
all Pretences of knowing mens spiritual state, & other secret
Things, not revealed in the word of God, or manifested by
the Events of Providence, by any supposed immediate Revelation, Impulse or Suggestion. I have always nauseated
the Presumption & folly of such as appeared forward to be
quick & peremptory in their decisions concerning the state
of mens souls, from a pretended extraordinary skill in the

secret methods of the spirits operation. And the older I have grown, the more & more has Experience and Observation of the Event of Things taught me the contemptibleness & Folly of such Pretences. I have much disliked the Tyranny of [of] Those who set up their own Experiences as a Rule to judge others by, and of such as insist on a particular account of the Time of Conversion, and of the order & method of their Experiences, in order to a cordial Embracing [of] Persons, who profess the main Principles or vertues wherein Godliness consists, & are of answerable conversation, in the arms of Charity as true Christians & Brethren in Christ. I have long born Testimony against these Things. I have ever been an Enemy to a separating, divisive, Factious, uncharitable spirit; and have exerted my self in many ways against such Things as They have abundantly appeared in the Country of late years. I have not set my self to oppose ministers, or to Encourage [?] a disaffection between ministers & People, under a Pretence of their not being converted, not being lively Preachers &c. I have heretofore lived in an happy union with the ministers of this neighbourhood; which I have industriously cultivated, and look'd upon as one of the special Blessings of my Life: But I fear this controversy has in some measure interrupted it, or at least the happy Fruits of it. A state of Controversy is peculiarly disagreable to me, and I look upon it as my great Calamity, & desire to take it as a Frown of Providence that should deeply humble me that I am obliged to enter into such a controversy [even] with my own People: I dreaded it greatly before it began, & nothing could make it tolerable to me, But that I have the Testimony of my Confidence that I could not avoid it, and so that 'tis an affliction that God lays upon me and calls me to bear.

I am often (and I don't know but pretty generally in the Country) represented as of a new & odd opinion with Respect to Terms of Christian Communion, and [that I am] as being for introducing a peculiar way of my own: whereas I don't perceive that I differ at all from the scheme of Dr. Watts in his Book entitled *The rational Foundation of a Christian Church, & the Terms of Christian Communion,* which he says is the common sentiment & Practice of all reformed Churches. I had not seen this Book of Dr. Watts's when I published what I have written on the subject; But yet I think my sentiments, as I have there express'd Them, are as exactly agreable to what he lays down, as If I had been his Pupil. nor do I at all go beyond what Dr. Doddridge plainly shews to be his sentiments in his *Rise & Progress of Religion,* & his *Sermons on Regeneration,* & in his *Paraphrase & notes on the N. Testament.* nor indeed Sir, [can I perceive] when I consider the sentiments you have express'd in your Letters to Maj. Pomroy & Mr. Billing, can I perceive but that They come exactly to the same Thing that I maintain. you suppose *The Sacraments are not converting ordinances; but that as seals of the covenant They presuppose conversion, especially in the adult; and that 'Tis visible Saintship, or in other words a credible Profession of Faith & Repentance, a solemn consent to the Gospel Covenant, Joined with a good conversation, and competent measure of Christian Knowledge, is what gives a Gospel Right to all sacred ordinances: but that it is necessary to those that come to these ordinances, & in those that profess a consent to the Gospel Covenant, that They are sincere in their Profession* or at least should think Themselves so. The great Thing which I have scrupled in the established method of this Churches Proceeding, & which I dare no longer go on in, is their publickly assenting to the form of words rehearsed on occasion of admission to the Communion, without pretending thereby to mean any such Thing as an hearty consent to the Terms of the Gospel Covenant, or to mean any such Faith or Repentance as belong to the Covenant of Grave, & are the grand Conditions of that Covenant; It being, at the same Time that the words are used, Their known & establish'd Principle, which They openly profess & proceed upon, that men may & ought to use these words & mean no such Thing, but something Else of a nature far inferiour, of which I think They have no distinct determinate notions, but something consistent with their knowing That They don't chuse God as their Chief Good, but love the world more than Him, and that They do not give Themselves up entirely to God, but make Reserves; and in short, knowing that they don't heartily consent to the Gospel Covenant but live still under the reigning Power of the Love of the World, and Enmity to God and Christ. So that the words of their publick Profession, according to Their openly established use, cease to be of the nature of any Profession of Gospel Faith & Repentance, or any proper Compliance with the Covenant; for 'tis their Profession that the words as used, mean no such Thing. The words used under these Circumstances do at least fail of being a *credible Profession of these Things.* I can conceive of no such vertue in a certain set of words, that 'tis proper, meerly on the making these sounds, to admit Persons to Christian Sacraments, without any Regard to any pretended meaning of these sounds: nor can I think that any Institution of Christ has establish'd any such Terms of admission into the Christian Church. It don't belong to the controversy between me & my People, how particular or large the Profession should be that is [should be] required. I should not chuse to be confined to exact Limits as to that matter; But rather than contend, I should content my self with a few words, briefly expressing the cardinal vertues or acts implied in a hearty compliance with the Covenant, made (as should appear by enquiry into the Persons doctrinal Knowledge) understandingly, if there were an external conversation agreable thereto. Yea I should think that such a Person solemnly making such a Profession, had a Right to be received as the object of a publick Charity, however

He Himself might scruple his own conversion, on account
of his not remembring the Time, not knowing the Method
of his Conversion, or finding so much remaining sin &c.
And if his own scruples did not hinder his coming to the
Lords Table, I should think the minister or Church had
no Right to debar such a Professour, tho' He should say
He did not think Himself converted: for I call that a Profession of Godliness, which is a Profession of the great
Things wherein Godliness consists; & not a Professing his
own opinion of his good Estate.

when I say in my Book that a *positive Charity* is requisite, my meaning has been misunderstood by some, as tho'
by *positive*, I had meant *peremptory*. whereas I meant no
more than *positive*, in opposition to a meer *negation* of a
contrary determination. I think there should [be] not only
be no evidence against a man but some positive exhibition
or visibility implying probability, or some worthiness of a
real act of the charitable Judgment of the Church in a
Persons Favour as a true Christian, agreable to his Profession. I think you express the very same Thing, when
you speak of a *credible* Profession as what entitles a man
to admission. *credible* in that which is worthy of *credit*
or *belief*.

Sir, If you write to my People your opinion of my Book
as you proposed in your Letter, I desire you would do it
before the Council that is to meet here on June 19. to
judge whether or no I ought immediately to be dismissed
from my Pastoral office. and I ask the Favour of you, of
sending me a copy of your Letter to Them, [or specially
directing Them to let me see what you write] otherwise
'tis probable I may never know what you write and that
the People will never see it, at least not before the Council,
unless it be truly in their Favour. It was not without some
difficulty that your last letter to Maj. P—— was communicated even to the Precinct, tho' you directed that it
should be communicated. However They yet stand to it

that you are on their side. — The state of this People is very unhappy. — I would not speak to their disparagement: I know it is a day of great Temptation with Them; and allowances must be made for Them on many accounts. — In your Letter to Mr. Billing, you say, Rev. Sir, that *He speaks as one that knows the Heart of a minister:* But there [are] but few that Know the Heart of a minister under my circumstances. — [But] It would be tedious, & would tire your Patience for me to give a particular account of the state of Things. But if you had fully known Them, & how ready a People in such a state are to catch at every word, from a man They have received such a Character of, and to make much of little Things, you would probably have forborn, [only] on so uncertain a Report of my Principles, to say to Them, *They might easily be reduced to an absurdity,* tho' it was only on [condition] supposition you had been rightly informed. — some Things which you have said have been improved to my disadvantage, both by ministers & People; tho' I confess without your having given Them much occasion.

I conclude with asking your fervent Prayers to the God of all Light & Grace for me under my great Troubles

I am

Honoured Sir, with much esteem & Respect,

your son & servant,

JONATHAN EDWARDS.

The Rev. Mr. Clark.

Another alternative to the Puritan practices was offered by the Separates. Their policy was one of exclusiveness usually associated with Jonathan Edwards. But as Ebenezer Frothingham makes quite clear in the following passage, the Separates did not agree with Edwards in all aspects of the question.

EBENEZER FROTHINGHAM

*The Articles of Faith and Practice, with the Covenant, That Is
Confessed by the Separate Churches of Christ in this Land. . . .*
Newport, 1750, pp. 33, 34, 36, 37, 38, 39, 40–42

In prosecuting this Discourse, we shall first endeavour to
prove the fifteenth Article before recited in this Book, which is,
that real Believers, and none but such, are Members of the true
Church of Jesus Christ, *&c.*

But we find the Work considerably shortned by one that we
trust the Truth will be receiv'd more freely from, without
Prejudice, *viz.* Mr. *Edwards,* in his late Book, entituled, 'An
Enquiry into the Qualifications for full Communion in the visible Church.' But we would observe to the Reader, that altho'
we don't join with Mr. *Edwards* in every particular Thing laid
down in the Book, yet as to the Substance of the Arguments
and Scriptures brought to prove that none have a Right to the
Lord's Supper but real Saints, and that there was no half-way
Covenant; we say, as to the Substance of the Arguments and
Scriptures brought by the Author to prove these Points, and
also the Duty of Saints visibly covenanting with God and each
other, and there frequently renewing the same, we do highly
esteem, as being agreeable to sound Doctrine, and the eternal
Standard of Truth; therefore we would heartily recommend
the Book (excepting some Particulars in it) to the serious Pe-
rusal of every Person of all Ranks and Denominations, earnestly
praying that the all-wise and merciful God would bless it, and
make it Instrumental of bringing the Saints in *New-England*
into the real Order of the Gospel, that so we may be of one
Heart, and brought into one Practice, in attending the Institutions of the Gospel of Jesus Christ. . . .

We would take Notice of the Author's horrid Reflection
cast upon the Wisdom and Sovereignty of God (however we
are apt to think it was done in Ignorance); for in his writing of
the Separate Errors, faith, Their lay Ordinations, their lay

Preaching, and publick Exhorting and Administering Sacraments. Therefore to use the like Form of Expressions as the
Author has himself in the like Case, pag. 124. we reply, and say
this Reflection is not so much against the Separates and lay
Teachers, as it is against the Holy Scriptures, which has mark'd
out such Men exactly as hath lately been ordain'd as Elders in
the separate or rising Churches of Jesus Christ in this Land, and
exactly such a Form of Ordination and Sacraments has been
attended to them, as the Holy Ghost has pointed out in the
sacred Scriptures of eternal Truth; but for the Proof of this
Assertion, we refer the Reader to what we shall proceed to
prove by and by. We now pass on to consider and enquire into
the Visibility that the Author holds as the Door of Admission
into the Church; and if it should so happen, that we should
prove from the Author's Writing, the same Visibility as the
Door of Admission into the visible Church as we hold, we
would hope that he and others may have an Occasion to reflect
upon themselves for marking us out by way of Reproach and
Contempt, as the only Persons in the Land that pretend to a pure
Church, when he and they hold to a visible Evidence of gracious
Sincerity, or real Saintship, even of that Sort of Saintship which
the Saints in Heaven have, see pag. 19. Now this we confess is
the Truth in fact; and we know not of one Saint that is in
regular Standing in any of the Separate Churches in the Land,
that hold to any fuller or further Evidence than this Testimony
is: And notwithstanding this clear Truth the Author has laid
down, yet by some other Passages, we are prone to think that
he don't understand himself, or else contradicts himself; which
brings us into a further Enquiry into this Visibility the Author
insists upon: And here first, we think the Author makes a
strange Mistake about stating his Visibility; for in pag. 19. he
holds a Visibility of real Saintship of that Sort which the Saints
in Heaven have; and in pag. 5 and 13, and elsewhere, he holds
that no Christian or Man can tell that another believes that Jesus
is the Messiah, or that a Person may be a Hypocrite, notwithstanding his Visibility of Saintship. Now if we understand the

Word Visibility, it is a making manifest and visible to the Observation, and Understanding the Thing requested; for Instance, suppose one should request of another to present before him a Sheep, and he should present a Goat: Now is the Sheep visible, or is it not? So again, if one should request the Fruit of an Apple Tree, and the Fruit of a Thorn Bush is presented, is the Apple visible or not? Surely no, nor is the Request answered: But on the contrary, if the Apple is presented, it is visibly seen and known, and more especially if it be tasted of; therefore to have a Thing visible that is requested, amounts to certain Knowledge of the Thing thus presented: For supposing an Hypocrite presents himself to join to a Church that holds a visible Evidence of real Saintship and gracious Sincerity, as Terms of Communion; now a Church holding strictly to these Terms, an Hypocrite can no ways get into the Church; and the Reason is, because no Hypocrite under Heaven has the Conditions required; and that that is not, cannot be. No Hypocrite, altho never so refin'd, has any Foundation laid to produce a Visibility of Saintship, by Reason that they have no gracious Sincerity, nor real Saintship. Again, the Author writes thus: 'In the same Manner, and no otherwise, I suppose that Christian Grace itself is a Qualification requisite in order to a proper solid Ground of a Right in a Person to come to the Christian Sacraments, pag. 4.' Now this is true; but if we don't mistake the Author (for he writes in a misterious Manner, backwards and forwards, about this Visibility), in his making a Distinction between a Person's Right to present himself to the Church for Communion, and the Church's Right to receive. In the same Page he writes a Profession of the Belief of a future State, and of reveal'd Religion, and some other Things that are Internal, and out of Sight, and a Visibility of these Things to the Eye of a Christian Judgment, is all relating to those Things that is requisite to give a Man a Right before the Church; but it is the real Existence of these things, that is what lays a proper and good foundation for his making this Profession, &c. By this we conclude, the Author means that the Church must receive in Members upon bare

Profession of Godliness, and the Doctrines of the Gospel, let them be Hypocrites or not, see pag. 7. And if this be the Case in fact, then a Door is open to stuff the Churches full of lying Hypocrites, twice as much as Mr. *Stoddard*'s Scheme, for he allowed Persons to come to the Lord's Supper, owning that they was unconverted, in order to get converting Grace: But this Scheme of the Author's, will gather a Church of a Number of abhor'd Hypocrites, that come with a solemn Lie before God and Man (an Expression which the Author frequently uses, and a Way of Lying he abundantly speaks against). We have abundant Reason to think (and more especially since we have had such a great Day of God's Grace of late Years), that there are Hundreds, if not Thousands in this Land, that have no more saving Grace than any profess'd Drunkard, or prayerless, loose, wicked Lives whatever, and yet at the same Time have had a common Work of the Spirit of God by Convictions, and some Illuminations, and can tell over a Form of Christian Experience by Rote, more correct than many real Saints and have an Head Knowledge of the Letter of the true Doctrines of the Gospel, and such a Measure of common restraining Grace, as to keep them in a legal moral Way of Profession and yet all this while, those Persons may be known to have no saving Grace, by Reason that they cannot produce any visible Fruits of a Union to Christ. *Matt.* 7, 18, 20, 21 ver. *A good Tree cannot bring forth evil Fruit, neither can a corrupt Tree bring forth good Fruit; wherefore by their Fruits ye shall know them. Not every one that saith unto me Lord, Lord,* &c. All the visible Fruits they bear, is from common restraining Grace, which Multitudes have, and confess it with their own Mouths that they are unconverted, and have not a Spark of real Charity; so they are like a sounding Brass, or tinkling Symbol. 1 *Cor.* 13 chap. 1 ver.

Observe if a Profession of Godliness only, with common restraining Grace, be the Church's Foundation to receive in Members upon, then the Case may be so, that a whole Church may be a Number of lying Hypocrites, and Heart Enemies to Jesus Christ, by Reason that a Profession of Godliness is all that is required (and this any Hypocrite can make), instead of visible Fruits of Godliness and true Piety. Jesus Christ saith of such Sort of Professors as we plead against, that they are of their Father the Devil. *John* 8. 44. *Ye art of your Father the Devil, and the Lusts of your Father ye will do.* Now can any Person think that a Number of the Devil's Children (altho' they may visibly profess to be Christ's Disciples), is Christ's Church, which he sets as a Seal upon his Heart and Arm; and to use the Author's Expressions in the like Case, which is, Be that Church of Christ which in the New Testament is denominated his City, his Temple, his Family, his Body, &c.

Still another way of dealing with membership was that favored by the "Liberal" wing of Puritanism (which generally had opposed the revival). Here this position is represented by Jonathan Mayhew.

JONATHAN MAYHEW
Christian Sobriety: Being Eight Sermons on Titus II. . . .
Boston, 1763, pp. 100–104, 108–111

It is therefore to be observed, in the next place, that Christian sobriety implies in it,

VI. An *external confession* of Christ's name, a profession of the religion which bears it, and an explicit dedication of One's self to the service and glory of God in him. No person of adult age has any right to be looked upon as a sober-minded or real Christian, till he has given reason for others to think him such, by making a christian profession in conformity to the order of the gospel, or the commandment of our Saviour, and the laws of his kingdom.   And here,

1. It is required, not only that you believe in Christ, but voluntarily, or by an act of your own, take upon yourselves the character of his disciples and followers, by "naming his name" in a solemn and public manner, or "before men"; thereby visibly devoting yourselves to God in him, and laying yourselves under obligation to conduct your selves in other re-

spects, as becomes the professed followers of him, who was "holy, harmless, undefiled, separate from sinners." The Lord Jesus Christ not only encourages such a public confession of him, by a gracious promise on one hand; but discountenances the neglect hereof by a most awful threatning on the other. "Whosoever shall confess me before men," saith he, "him shall the Son of Man also confess before the angels of God. But he that denieth me before men, shall be denied before the angels of God." [4] In another evangelist it is, — "before my Father which is in heaven." [5] He says, nearly to the same purpose, elsewhere. — Whosoever shall be ashamed of me, and of my words, of him shall the Son of man be ashamed, when he shall come in his own glory and his Father's, and of the holy angels." [6] These are very solemn warnings against disowning Christ, his name or "his words," even in times of sore trial and persecution for righteousness sake; to which times they more particularly refer. But, to be ashamed of, to disown or to neglect confessing them, when there is nothing of that sort to be feared, is doubtless far more criminal and dangerous. It is manifest from the whole current of the new-testament, that the faith of the heart is to be accompanied with the confession of the tongue; and that as necessary to salvation, except in extraordinary cases. "If thou shalt confess with thy mouth the Lord Jesus," says the apostle, "and shalt believe *in thine heart* that God hath raised him from the dead, thou shalt be saved. For with the heart man believeth unto righteousness, and with the mouth confession is made unto salvation." [7] Indeed, if any who know this to be the will and commandment of Christ respecting them that believe on him, the contempt or wilful neglect thereof, is absolutely inconsistent with a sincere regard to him and his authority: It is, in its nature, inconsistent with such a faith in him as the scripture speaks of as saving; which faith respects him as truly in his regal, as in his prophetic or sacerdotal character. But,

---

[4] Luke 12. 8, 9.   [5] Matt. 10th Chap.   [6] Luke 9. 26.
[7] Rom. x. 9, 10.

2. Tho' it is positively injoined upon those who believe in Christ, to confess him before men; yet it is not to be supposed necessary, or the thing intended hereby, that persons should stand up in the midst of an assembly, and, *vivá voce,* or in express words uttered by themselves, declare their faith in him. For some cannot even *speak* at all, and much less in such a public manner. Neither can it be supposed necessary for them to profess their repentance, faith and experiences in a long writing, under their hands; — a common practice formerly in this country, but growing daily more and more into disuse; and not without sufficient reason, as being attended with divers inconveniences, which need not be particularly mentioned. Therefore,

3. Nothing more, or farther, can be supposed necessary as to this matter, than that people should, in a solemn, public manner, and by some sign, or significant gesture, commonly understood, make such a declaration of their faith in Christ; signifying their consent to the covenant of grace established in him, and their resolution, by the help of God, to walk in all the commandments and ordinances of the Lord, blameless; or to conduct themselves in all respects according to the laws of Christ's kingdom. This may be effectually done, without any speaking or writing on their part, in public. And as nothing beyond this can reasonably be supposed to be required, by "confessing Christ before men"; so neither can any thing short of it be supposed to come up to the thing really intended thereby, in any natural construction of the words, or in consistency with the practice of the christian church from the earliest times. . . .

5. There is a considerable number of those that may be justly accounted young men, tho' unmarried, who, in order to obtain baptism for their children, have made a profession of their faith in Christ, and solemnly bound themselves to observe *all* the laws of his kingdom; and yet turn their backs upon the Lord's table from year to year, as if this were no christian institution; — as tho' Christ had never said, "This do in remembrance of me"; and as tho' the inspired apostle had not said,

"As oft as ye eat of this bread, and drink of this cup, ye do shew the Lord's death, *till he come.*" It is not very easy to reconcile this neglect, with the supposition of your having been *sincere* and *in earnest,* when you engaged to obey all Christ's known commandments and institutions; — upon supposition that you allow this to be one of them, as you cannot deny it to be. I have often, and very particularly shewn what your duty is in this respect; tho' with much less success than was desired. However, I will not be weary or discouraged in reminding you of it; hoping that the time will come, when what is seriously said to you upon this head, will be as seriously attended to; and have a proper influence upon your practice: Which will be a better evidence of your being truly soberminded, than any that you can well give, while you habitually absent yourselves from the fellowship of Christ's church and people in one of his ordinances.

INDEED, if *unchristian* terms of christian communion are insisted on in any church or churches, your not being incorporated with them, provided it is solely for this reason, will not be your fault, but that of the imposers of such terms. Nor can it be denied, that there has been a great deal of this kind of antichristian imposition and tyranny practised in different ages; particularly in respect of *creeds,* or *articles* of faith. For, instead of being contented with such a simple, plain and apostolic confession as this, "I believe that *Jesus Christ is the Son of God*" [8]; or even with a general and serious profession of faith in the holy scriptures as the word of God; many churches have imperiously required an explicit profession of unscriptural articles of faith, as the pretended "form of sound words"; tho' almost barbarous enough, perhaps, both in expression and sentiment, at once to wound the ear, affront the sense, and shock the humanity of an *Hottentot!*

BUT, surely, it is time that all protestants, especially protestant-dissenters, should make the holy scriptures the standard of a sound faith and christian practice, in opposition to ALL

[8] Acts VIII: 37

OTHER *forms of sound words;* as some are pleased to mis-call
the reveries of poor crazy monks and lunaticks, half-distracted
schoolmen, superannuated enthusiasts, and proud, factious, ava-
ritious zealots for a party, pretending to make black white, and
white black; and then scolding at, and cursing all the world,
that would not implicitly believe their unholy ravings, and
submit to them as the true, uncorrupted *catholic faith!* — *God,*
in his own time, which is approaching, will put an end to all
these antichristian usurpations in his church. Christ's "fan is in
his hand, and he will thoro'ly purge his floor." And happy is it
for those who, in the mean while, neither exercise such tyranny
over others, nor suffer under it; at once allowing to all, and
enjoying themselves, that just and reasonable "liberty, where-
with Christ has made his disciples FREE from every such yoke
of bondage.

The Great Awakening, by breaking down ecclesiastical unity and fragmenting both denominations and individual churches, ultimately produced a need for practical toleration and a theoretical principle — the
separation of church and state — which justified the practice. The initial
impetus for both toleration and separation came from radical New Lights,
such as the Connecticut Separates who wrote the following petition.

*Isaac Backus on Church, State, and Calvinism: Pamphlets, 1754–
1789,* William G. McLoughlin, ed.
                    Cambridge, Mass., The Belknap Press of Harvard University,
                                                        1968, pp. 485–486

[*Petition of the Separates of Massachusetts to the General
Court, June 7, 1749*]

To His Excellency William Shirley Esqr. Captn. Generall
Governour in Chief In & Over His Majesties Province of Massachusetts Bay in New England, the Honl. His Majesties Council with the House of Representatives in Generall Court Assembled May 1749. The Representation & Petition of John Pain

& Samuel Peck of Rehoboth in the County of Bristoll in the Province And others of the Inhabitants of sd. Province: Many of Whome are Free Men of this Province and all of them Lege Subjects to His Royall Majesty King George the Second whom we Pray GOD long to Preserve. We whose Names are hereunto Subsribed humbly Sheweth that GOD hath [given] to every Man an Unalianable Right in Matters of His Worship to [act] for himself as his Conscience reseves [receives] the Rule from GOD & hath Blessed [those] that hath appeared to stand uprightly for the Liberty of Conscience in all Ages and Perticularly our fore Fathers who left their Pleasant Native Land for an [empty] houlling Wilderness full of Savage Men & Beasts that they might have Liberty of Conscience & they found the Marcifull & Faithful GOD was not a Wilderness [to them] but drove out the Saviges & Planted Chhs. [Churches] & Colonies: Also gave them Favour in the Sight of their Kings & Queens so that their Majesties granted to & in their Subjects in this Province with a Charter in which among other great Favours Liberty of Consciance is granted to all Christians except Papists. Notwithstanding this Liberty granted to us which wee Desire to Bless GOD for [&] Pray that we may rightly Improve the Same; Yet therr is some Laws called Ecclesiastical Laws which are so Understood by them that have the Execution of the Same that [if we?] Pass not under the Denomination of Churchmen or of the Church of England or AnnaBaptists or Quakers or do not Worship on the Sabbath with the [major] Part of the Town or Precinct whare We Live which we Cannot in Conscience do; Yet they by these Laws Imprison Some & put some in the Stock & also take away Some of our Goods & Chattles to maintaine their Minnesters which we Should [have] to serve GOD and honnour the King with; & this Notwithstanding we meet [?] in our severall Towns & worship God in Spirit & in Truth and Injoy Him [in His] Ordinances & have the Gospell of our Deer Lord Jesus Christ Preached to us without their Charge or Coast [Cost] & as these Oppressions being Still carried on among us; Your Honnours Petitioneurs humbly Pray that your

Honours [be] the happy Instruments in the Hand of GOD of
Onbinding these Heavy Burdens & letting the Oppressed goe
free by Enacting Universal Liberty or forbidding the Execution of s[ai]d Ecclesiastical Laws that are or may be to the
Debarring of any in this Province of the Liberties granted by
GOD & tollerated by our King and we as in Duety Bound Shall
ever Pray

JOHN PAINE
SAMUEL PECK
[*and 181 others*]

The following petition from the Presbyterian Synod of New York gives an
example of the impetus provided by the revival for the founding of new
universities.

Records of the Presbyterian Church, U.S.A., W. H. Roberts, ed.
Philadelphia, 1904, 55–57

To the very venerable and honourable the moderator and
other members of the General Assembly of the Church of Scotland, to meet at Edinburgh, May, 1754. The petition of the
Synod of New York, convened at Philadelphia, October 3,
1753, humbly showeth:

That a college has been lately erected in the province of New
Jersey by his majesty's royal charter, in which a number of
youth has been already educated, who are now the instruments
of service to the church of God; and which would be far more
extensively beneficial were it brought to maturity. That after
all the contributions that have been made to the said college,
or can be raised in these parts, the fund is far from being sufficient for the erection of proper buildings, supporting the president and tutors, furnishing a library, and defraying other
necessary expenses; that the trustees of said college, who are
zealous and active to promote it for the public good, have already sent their humble petition to this venerable house for
some assistance in carrying on so important a design; and also

petitioned this Synod to appoint two of their members, the Rev. Messrs. Gilbert Tennent and Samuel Davies, to undertake a voyage to Europe in behalf of said college.

Your petitioners, therefore, most heartily concur in the said petition of the trustees to the Reverend Assembly, and appoint the said Messrs. Tennent and Davies to be their commissioners for that purpose. . . .

In the colonies of New York, New Jersey, Pennsylvania, Maryland, Virginia, and Carolina, a great number of congregations have been formed upon the Presbyterian plan, which have put themselves under the Synodical care of your petitioners, who conform to the constitution of the Church of Scotland, and have adopted her standards of doctrine, worship, and discipline. There are also large settlements lately planted in various parts, particularly in North and South Carolina, where multitudes are extremely desirous of the ministrations of the gospel; but they are not yet formed into congregations, and regularly organized for want of ministers.

These numerous bodies of people, dispersed so wide through so many colonies, have repeatedly made the most importunate applications to your petitioners, for ministers to be sent among them; and your petitioners have exerted themselves to the utmost for their relief, both by sending their members and candidates to officiate some time among them, and using all practicable measures for the education of pious youth for the ministry.

But alas! notwithstanding these painful endeavours, your petitioners have been utterly incapable to make sufficient provision for so many shepherdless flocks; and those that come hundreds of miles crying to them for some to break the bread of life among them, are often obliged to return in tears, with little or no relief, by reason of the scarcity of ministers.

Though every practicable expedient, which the most urgent necessity could suggest, has been used to prepare labourers for this extensive and growing harvest; yet the number of ministers in this Synod is far from being equal to that of the congregations under their care. Though sundry of them have taken the pastoral charge of two or three congregations for a time, in order to lessen the number of vacancies; and though sundry youth have lately been licensed, ordained, and settled in congregations, that were before destitute; yet there are no less than forty vacant congregations at present under the care of this Synod, besides many more which are incapable at present to support ministers; and the whole colony of North Carolina, where numerous congregations of Presbyterians are forming, and where there is not one Presbyterian minister settled.

The great number of vacancies in the bounds of this Synod, is owing, partly, to the new settlements lately made in various parts of this continent, partly to the death of sundry ministers belonging to this Synod, but principally to the small number of youth educated for the ministry, so vastly disproportionate to the numerous vacancies; and unless some effectual measures can be taken for the education of proper persons for the sacred character, the churches of Christ in these parts must continue in the most destitute circumstances, wandering shepherdless and forlorn through this wilderness, thousands perishing for lack of knowledge, the children of God hungry and unfed, and the rising age growing up in a state little better than that of heathenism, with regard to the public ministrations of the gospel.

The numerous inconveniences of a private, and the many important advantages of a public education are so evident, that we need not inform this venerable assembly of them, who cannot but be sensible from happy experience, of the many extensive benefits of convenient colleges.

The difficulty, (and in some cases impossibility,) of sending youth, two, three, four, or five hundred miles or more, to the colleges in New England, is also evident at first sight. Now it is from the college of New Jersey only, that we can expect a remedy of these inconveniences; it is to *that* your petitioners look for the increase of their number; it is on *that* the Presbyterian churches, through the six colonies above mentioned, principally depend for a supply of accomplished ministers; from *that* has been obtained considerable relief already, notwithstanding the many disadvantages that unavoidably attend it in its present infant state; and from *that* may be expected a sufficient supply when brought to maturity.

Your petitioners, therefore, most earnestly pray, that this very reverend Assembly would afford the said college all the countenance and assistance in their power. The young daughter of the Church of Scotland, helpless and exposed in this foreign land, cries to her tender and powerful mother for relief. The cries of ministers oppressed with labours, and of congregations famishing for want of the sincere milk of the word, implore assistance. And were the poor Indian savages sensible of their own case, they would join in the cry, and beg for more missionaries to be sent to propogate the religion of Jesus among them.

Now as the college of New Jersey appears the most promising expedient to redress these grievances, and to promote religion and learning in these provinces, your petitioners most heartily concur with the trustees, and humbly pray, that an act may be passed by this venerable and honourable Assembly, for a national collection in favour of said college. And your petitioners as in duty bound shall ever pray, &c.

Proponents of revival always pointed to "moral reformation" as a principal accomplishment. Not all observers could find convincing evidence of reform, as the following remarks by the Carolina Anglican missionary, Charles Woodmason, indicate.

The Carolina Backcountry on the Eve of the Revolution: The Journal and Other Writings of Charles Woodmason, Anglican Itinerant, Richard J. Hooker, ed.
Chapel Hill, University of North Carolina Press, 1953, pp. 95–100

But surely, if Persons have received more and better Edification by resorting to the Schism Shop, then by continuing constant in Well doing at their own Chapel certainly it will display it Self in their Lives and Manners. This is the Test by which We must try the Validity of these Assertions — And

therefore I hope it will not be thought invidious if I enter
into a few Particulars. Because I hear so much Talk about
Conversion, certainly there must be some very Great Reformation of Morals among You: But I would not have Te Deum
sung before the Victory be gain'd.

You doubtless will allow, That keeping Holy the Lords day,
is a positive Command of God, and enjoin'd by the Laws of
this Land — And that Two Years past, it was rather more pro-
fan'd than any other day of the Week — and I would enquire
if it is not so still? It may be replied, That it is not — That
there is not that frolicing, feasting and Rioting as formerly.
But this I deny. For as my Station leads me to travel over most
Parts of the Country, and ofttimes on Sundays, as well as other
Days, I do aver, that there is little or no Reformation of Manners on this Head save in some few Environs of a Meeting
House, or among the Cohee Settlers — For the same riding the
Woods, Shooting Cattle Hunting — driving Waggons, Hogs
Horses — Travelling to and fro — Fishing — Fowling — Trap-
ping — Taverning, Swimming and Bathing, and various Field
and Domestic Matters, are carried on, and followed up as
usual. Nor can I perceive any Reform: So far from it, That
the Sabbath is not so regularly observ'd, as when You us'd
statedly to resort to Church: but since quitting of the Church,
the Sabbath is but seldom observ'd — for we see none resort to
any Place of Worship, but when some Itinerant Babler, or Va-
grant Ignorant Bellweather comes to a Meeting House and then
the Silly Herd run in Droves to listen to what none can compre-
hend and this for greater Edification. If therefore staying at
Home, Sleeping and Lounging privately tipling and wantoning,
be hallowing the Lords Day, I will acknowledge that in this
Sense it is *highly* sanctified — tho' I think it would more ra-
tionally and more religiously be so, would People resort to
their proper Churches to hear the Word of God solemnly
read, and their Duty explain'd to them in a sober, sensible and
judicious Manner.

*   *   *

It may be reply'd to me, That altho' People do stay at home, and not come to Chapel on those Sundays when there is no Sermon at the Meeting Yet that they employ themselves in Religious Exercises, and Works of Edification: What Works? — In Singing of Hymns and Spiritual Songs — whereby their Hearts are greatly inflam'd with Divine Love and Heav'nly Joy, and makes the H[oly] G[host] be shed abroad in their Hearts. This is very fine *Talking:* I could wish that all the *Doings* too, were equally Innocent. But let me say, that these Assemblies at Private Houses for Singing Hymns, is very reprehensible. First because People may assemble in this Place, and Sing, and then no Scandal would arise, and 2dly The Hymns commonly sung, had far better be thrown into the Fire. I have seen many of them — Which are not only execrable in Point of Versification, but withal full of Blasphemy, Nonsense, and Incoherence. No Edification therefore can spring from such Singing. Withal should it be said, that they thus meet because these Hymns and Tunes are not permitted in the Church — I answer That as to the Tunes, the Clerk is the Person concern'd Who is both able and willing to gratify any in Choice of Tunes; And as for Hymns We do not disallow of them, provided they be Solemn, Sublime, Elegant and Devout — Fit to be offer'd up to the Throne of Grace — And such can be furnish'd to any Religious Society, desirous of them.

The best Things are most liable to Abuse — And these Singing Matches lie under the Imputation of being only Rendezvous of Idlers, under the Mask of Devotion. Meetings for Young Persons to carry on Intrigues and Amours. For all Classes of Villains, and the Vicious of both Sexes to make Assignations; and for others to indulge themselves in Acts of Intemperance and Wantoness, So that these Religious Societies are Evil spoken off, and therefore ought to be abolished conformable to what was done in the Primitive Times. The first Christians us'd to assemble at Nights, at the Tombs of the Martyrs, and there sing Hymns and perform Prayers. But as this gave Offence to the Heathens, and occasion'd the whole Body to be

censur'd for the irregularities of a Few it was judged proper
to abolish these Nocturnal Meetings: And this Act of the
Primitive Church ought to be a Rule to us at present: For it is
rather better to decline an Innocent Duty that may be productive of some Good, rather than to have it perverted by base
Minds to many Purposes of Evil.

*   *   *

We will further enquire if Lascivousness, or Wantoness,
Adultery or Fornication [are] less common than formerly,
before the Arrival of these *Holy* Persons? Are there fewer
Bastards born? Are more Girls with their Virginity about
them, Married, than were heretofore? The Parish Register will
prove the Contrary: There are rather more Bastards, more
Mullatoes born than before. Nor out of 100 Young Women
that I marry in a Year have I seen, or is there seen, Six but what
are with Child? And this as Common with the Germans on
other Side the River, as among You on this Side: So that a
Minister is accounted as a Scandalous Person for even coming
here to marry such People, and for baptizing their Bastard
Children as the Law obliges Me to register All Parties who are
Married, and all Children Born. This occasions such Numbers
(especially of the Saints) to fly into the next Province, and up
to the German Ministers and any where to get Married, to prevent their being register'd, as therefrom the Birth of their
Children would be trac'd: And as for Adulteries, the present
State of most Persons around 9/10 of whom now labour under
a filthy Distemper (as is well known to all) puts that Matter
out of all Dispute and shews that the Saints however outwardly
Precise and Reserved are not one Whit more Chaste than
formerly, and possibly are more privately Vicious.

And nothing more leads to this Than what they call their
Love Feasts and Kiss of Charity. To which Feasts, celebrated at
Night, much Liquor is privately carried, and deposited on the
Roads, and in Bye Paths and Places. The Assignations made on
Sundays at the Singing Clubs, are here realized. And it is no
wonder that Things are as they are, when many Young Persons

have 3. 4. 5. 6 Miles to walk home in the dark Night, with Convoy, thro' the Woods? Or staying perhaps all Night at some Cabbin (as on Sunday Nights) and sleeping together either doubly or promiscuously? Or a Girl being mounted behind a Person to be carried home, or any wheres. All this indeed contributes to multiply Subjects for the King in this frontier Country, and so is wink'd at by the Magistracy and Parochial Officers but at same time, gives great Occasion to the Enemies of Virtue, to triumph, for Religion to be scandalized and brought into Contempt; For all Devotion to be Ridicul'd, and in the Sequel, will prove the Entire banishment and End of all Religion — Confusion — Anarchy and ev'ry Evil Work will be the Consequence of such Lewdness and Immorality. . . .

One of the most controversial aspects of evangelical pietism is whether it was revolutionary or quietistic in its impetus. While pietism's otherworldliness is obvious, it frequently had as well an apocalyptic vision of salvation which had curiously radical overtones. The following selection from the writings of Joseph Bellamy (a follower of Jonathan Edwards) illustrates this theme.

JOSEPH BELLAMY

The Works of the Rev. Joseph Bellamy, D.D. Late of Bethlem, Connecticut.

New York, 1811, I, pp. 513–516

The periods past, that have been so dark, ought to be considered as introductory to this bright and glorious scene, and in various respects as preparatory thereto.

An apostate race, who had joined with the fallen angels in a course of rebellion against the Governor of the universe, might justly have been forsaken of God, and given up to a state of perfect darkness and wo, from generation to generation, entirely under the power of the prince of darkness. What has happened, in dark ages past, may help us a little to realize what might justly always have been the woeful state of a fallen world. We have had a specimen of the dreadful nature and tendency of satan's government, in all the idolatry, wickedness, and wo, which have filled the world. And we have seen a little what is in the heart of fallen man, who have slain the Lord's prophets, crucified his Son, and shed the blood of thousands, yea, of millions of his servants. And what has happened may help us to realize a little what must have been the state of a fallen world, if grace had never interposed. At the same time it hath appeared, after the best contrived experiments have been sufficiently tried, that it is not in the heart of fallen man to repent, nor can he be brought to it by any external means whatsoever; whereby the absolute necessity of the interposition of supernatural grace hath been set in the most glaring light. And now, if after all, God should effectually interpose, destroy the influence of satan, scatter the darkness which fills the world, recover mankind to God, and cause truth and righteousness at last to prevail; it would appear to be altogether of God, of his own mere self-moving goodness and sovereign grace. And after so long and sore a bondage, mankind will be the more sensible of the greatness of the deliverance. Nor can it ever be said by a proud and haughty world, "we did not need the influences of divine grace to bring us right;" when all other methods had been sufficiently tried, and tried in vain. But God may justly say, "what could have been done more to reclaim mankind, that I have not done? And to what purpose would it have been, to have taken one step further? I tried them enough. There was no hope. Their heart was a heart of stone. Therefore, behold, I, even I, will take away the heart of stone, and give an heart of flesh; and an apostate world shall be ashamed and confounded, and shall never open their mouth, when I shall do all these things for them."

We are apt to wonder why these glorious days should be so long delayed, if God indeed intends such mercy to men. But God, infinitely wise, knows what is best; knows how to conduct the affairs of the universe; knows when is the fittest time to introduce this glorious state of things; knows when matters will be all ripened, and every thing in the moral world prepared; so that this glorious day may be ushered in to the best advantage, in a manner most suited to honour God and his Son, to humble a haughty world, and to disappoint satan most grievously, after all his wily schemes, great success, and high expectations: I say, God knows when this will be. And this is the very time he has fixed upon for this glorious work. . . .

It therefore becomes all the followers of Christ, in their several spheres, under a firm belief of these things, to be of good courage, and exert themselves to the utmost, in the use of all proper means, to suppress error and vice of every kind, and promote the cause of truth and righteousness in the world; and so be workers together with God.

If one stood at the head of this glorious army, which has been in the wars above these five thousand years, and has lived through many a dreadful campaign, and were allowed to make a speech to these veteran troops upon his glorious theme, he might lift up his voice, and say, "Hail, noble heroes! brave followers of the Lamb! Your general has sacrificed his life in this glorious cause, and spoiled principalities and powers on the cross! and now he lives and reigns. He reigns on high, with all power in heaven and earth in his hands. Your predecessors, the Prophets, Apostles, and Martyrs, with undaunted courage, have marched into the field of battle, and conquered dying! and now reign in heaven! behold, ye are risen up in their room, are engaged in the same cause, and the time of the last general battle draws on, when a glorious victory is to be won. And, although many a valiant soldier may be slain in the field; yet the army shall drive all before them at last. And satan being conquered, and all the powers of darkness driven out of the field, and confined to the bottomless pit, ye shall reign with Christ a thousand years; reign in love and peace, while truth and righteousness ride triumphant through the earth. Wherefore lay aside every weight, and, with your hearts wholly intent on this grand affair, gird up your loins, and with all the spiritual weapons of faith, prayer, meditation, watchfulness, &c. with redoubled zeal and courage, fall on your spiritual enemies. Slay every lust that yet lurks within, as knowing your domestic foes are the most dangerous: and with gentleness, meekness, and wisdom,

by your holy conduct, your pious examples, your kind instructions, your friendly admonitions, spread the savour of divine
knowledge all around you, as ye are scattered here and there
through a benighted world; labouring to win souls to Christ,
to induce the deluded followers of satan to desert his camp,
and enlist as volunteers under your prince, MESSIAH. And if
the powers of darkness should rally all their forces, and a general battle through all the Christian world come on; O, love not
your lives to the death! Sacrifice every earthly comfort in the
glorious cause! Sing the triumphs of your victorious general in
prisons and at the stake! And die courageously, firmly believing the cause of truth and righteousness will finally prevail."

Surely it is infinitely unbecoming the followers of Him who
is *King of kings and Lord of lords,* to turn aside to earthly pursuits, or to sink down in unmanly discouragements, or to give
way to sloth and effeminacy, when there is so much to be done,
and the glorious day is coming on. How should those who
handle the pen of the writer, exert themselves to explain and vin-
dicate divine truths, and paint the Christian religion in all its native glories! How should the pulpit be animated, from sabbath
to sabbath, with sermons full of knowledge and light, full of
spirit and life, full of zeal for God, and love to men, and tender
pity to infatuated sinners! Christ loves to have his ministers
faithful, whether the wicked will hear or not. And let pious
parents be unwearied in their prayers for, and instructions of
their children, and never faint under any discouragements; as
knowing, that Christ is exalted to give repentance and remission of sins, and can do it for whom he will. Bring your children and friends, with all their spiritual diseases, and lay them
at his feet; as once they did their sick, when this kind Saviour
dwelt on earth. Let pious persons of every age, and in every
capacity, awake from sleep, and arise from the dead, and live
and act worthy their glorious character and high expectations;
and in their several stations exert themselves to the utmost to
promote the Redeemer's glorious cause. Let this age do their
share, as David, although the temple was not to be built in his
day, yet exerted himself to lay up materials for that magnificent

edifice, on which his heart was intently set; as knowing, that in his son's day it would be set up in all its glory. So let us rise up, and with the greatest alacrity contribute our utmost towards this building, this living temple, this temple all made of lively stones, of stones alive, in which God is to dwell, and which will infinitely exceed in glory the temple of Solomon, that was built of dead timber and lifeless stones. And let this be our daily prayer, an answer to which we may be assured of, whatever other requests are denied us, *our Father which art in heaven,* &c. *for thine is the kingdom, the power, and the glory, for ever.* AMEN.

One manifestation of ecumenical cooperation resulting from the Awakening was the "New Building" erected in Philadelphia in 1740 to provide a meetinghouse for itinerant preachers. The following documents offer some notion of ecumenicalism and the constraints within which it operated in eighteenth-century America.

The Autobiography of Benjamin Franklin, L. W. Labaree, et al., eds.
New Haven, Yale University Press, 1964, 175–176

In 1739 arriv'd among us from England the Rev. Mr. White-fiel, who had made himself remarkable there as an itinerant Preacher. He was at first permitted to preach in some of our Churches; but the Clergy taking a Dislike to him, soon refus'd him their Pulpits and he was oblig'd to preach in the Fields. The Multitudes of all Sects and Denominations that attended his Sermons were enormous, and it was matter of Speculation to me who was one of the Number, to observe the extraordinary Influence of his Oratory on his Hearers, and how much they admir'd and respected him, notwithstanding his common Abuse of them, by assuring them they were naturally *half Beasts and half Devils.* It was wonderful to see the Change soon made in the Manners of our Inhabitants; from being thoughtless or indifferent about Religion, it seem'd as if all the World were growing Religious; so that one could not walk thro' the Town in an Evening without Hearing Psalms sung in

different Families of every Street. And it being found incon-
venient to assemble in the open Air, subject to its Inclemencies,
the Building of a House to meet in was no sooner propos'd and
Persons appointed to receive Contributions, but sufficient Sums
were soon receiv'd to procure the Ground and erect the Building which was 100 feet long and 70 broad, about the Size of
Westminster-hall; and the Work was carried on with such
Spirit as to be finished in a much shorter time than could have
been expected. Both House and Ground were vested in Trustees, expressly for the Use of any Preacher of any religious Persuasion who might desire to say something to the People of
Philadelphia, the Design in building not being to accommodate
any particular Sect, but the Inhabitants in general, so that even
if the Mufti of Constantinople were to send a Missionary to
preach Mahometanism to us, he would find a Pulpit at his
Service. (The Contributions being made by People of different
Sects promiscuously, Care was taken in the Nomination of
Trustees to avoid giving a Predominancy to any Sect, so that
one of each was appointed, viz. one Church of England-man,
one Presbyterian, one Baptist, one Moravian, &c.).

DIETMAR ROTHERMUND
*The Layman's Progress: Religious and Political Experience in
Colonial Pennsylvania, 1740–1770.*
Philadelphia, 1961, pp. 145–151

["*Title of the Deed. Declaration of Trust of the New meeting
house and Parish school with the Lot of Ground thereby belonging —*"]

This indenture made 14 Nov.ᵐ 1740 Between E. W[ooley]
etc. of the one Part and G[eorge] W[hitefield] etc. other Part.
Whereas by Indenture bearing the date the 15th day of September last past between I. P[rice] of Philadelphia and his
wife she being the only daughter and Heir of J. C. (?) late of
Philadelphia deceased. . . .

And whereas a considerable number of Persons of different Denominations in Religion have united their Endeavours to erect a large Building upon the Land above described and mentioned to be granted intending that the same shall be applied to the use of a Charity School for the Instruction of Poor Children gratis in usefull Literature and the knowledge of the Christian Religion and also that the same used as a House of Public Worship. And it is agreed that the use of the said Building be under the Direction of certain Trustees viz. that the before G[eorge] W[hitefield] etc. and other Persons to be appointed by them or the majority of them and the survivors and the majority of such survivors from Time to Time as occasion shall require so that the number of Trustees do not exceed the number —— [blank] nor be less than —— [blank] at any time if it can be conveniently prevented. Which Trustees before named and hereafter to be chosen are from time to time to appoint fit and able schoolmasters and schoolmistresses for the service of the said School and introduce such Protestant ministers to preach the Gospel in the said Houses as they shall judge to be sound in their Principles Zealous and faithful in the Discharge of their Duty and acquainted with the Religion of the Heart and Experimental Piety without any Regard to those Distinctions or differing Sentiments in lesser matters which have to the scandal of Religion unhappily divided real Christians etc. Now this Indenture witnesseth that they the said E. W[ooley] etc. for the more effectual preserving the Land and the Building thereon and hereafter to be erected for the affirmed use do by these presents declare and agree that the said E. W[ooley] etc. and their Heirs will from henceforth stand seized of and interested in the above granted Land and Premises and the Building thereon erected and to be in trust for the above named G[eorge] W[hitefield] etc. the survivors and survivor of them and their Heirs of such survivors so that for the only proper use benefit and behalf the said G[eorge] W[hitefield] etc. and the survivors etc. . . .

And the said E. W[ooley] etc. . . . covenant and promise to G[eorge] W[hitefield] etc. . . . that they assume the proper cost and charges in the Law and upon the reasonable degree and Demand of the said G[eorge] W[hitefield] etc. . . . will grant and convey in due Form of Law the above mentioned Land and Premises with the appt., and every Part and Parcel thereof to each Person or Persons so to and for such uses and purposes and in such Manners as they the said G[eorge] W[hitefield] etc. or the Major Part of them . . . shall by writing under their Hands or Hand subscribed in the Presence of 2 Witnesses nominated and appointed. And the said E. W[ooley] etc. . . . do further covenant . . . [that they will not do] any act . . . whereby the above mentioned Premises may be charged Incumbered or evicted or whereby the Trust hereby declared may be conveyed, defeated or made void without the consent of the said G[eorge] W[hitefield] etc. or the Major part of them. . . .

In Testimony whereof the said Parties to these Presents have interchangeably set their Hands and Seals thereonto, dated the Day and Year first above written. . . .

Article No. 10 of the Articles of the Trustees

We do also give our Assent and Consent to the 9th, 10th, 11th, 12th, 13th and 17th articles of the Church of England as explained by the Calvinists in their literal and grammatical sense without any Equivocation, whatsoever, we mention therein particular because they are a summary of the foregoing articles. We believe all that are sound in the Faith agree in those whatever other Points they may differ in.

[Gilbert Tennent to George Whitefield, June 5, 1742.]

You never did in all your life [anything] of such dreadful tendency to the Church of God as your favoring that sect of Enthusiastical Herreticks [Moravians]. . . .

O Brother you will pull down with your one hand what you built with your other while you commend the Moravian deceivers Mr. Brogden [sic] has refused Mr. Blair's Brother to sign the Articles of the New Building in order to preach in it. I hear he wants to introduce the Moravians into it and to have the Articles altered, but whether would not this be to make the New Building a Bable of Confusion and to impose a manifest wrong upon the encouragers of it many of whom have gone upon the plan of the Articles and whether it would not contradict the primary design of this house which was to encourage Calvinistical Doctrines I leave you to determine.

[*George Whitefield to the Trustees of the New Building; Edinburgh, Sept. 19, 1742.*]

I hear there are strange confusions in Philadelphia. I cannot say they surprize, stagger me at all, because I am persuaded that our great & compassionate high Priest will overrule them all for good. Let us wait upon him in the spirit of meekness. It gave me some concern my Dear Brethren when I heard Mr. Blair was refused to sign the Articles of the New Building and that there was in all likelyhood a design to alter the Articles to introduce the Moravian Brethren. This I think will be productive of much disorder and make that house a mere Bable. What a value I have for the Moravians is very well known but I think it unjust and as well as imprudent to have a whole set of Articles altered to introduce them. This will be a notorious proof that they are enemies to the Doctrines of the Protestant reformed churches and shew (whatever they may say to the contrary) they do thrust themselves into other Men's labours. I cannot think the Brethren will put you upon this. If they do I justly charge them of making a breach between them and me, now we are friendly, one towards another. You know my Dear Brethren that house was built for me and other experimental Calvinistical preachers — And now to alter the Articles on such an account is too much like the people turning Calvin out of Geneva, though in a few years after they were glad of their Calvin again. I am persuaded such a procedure will hurt the common cause. It is by no means proper that two sets of men should preach in the same place unless they are agreed in all points of Doctrine and manner of preaching. It will be better to have different place(s) of preaching as we have in London. This may be done and yet a sweet amiable Christian fellowship kept up amongst each other. The Moravians in some things greatly err notwithstanding I love them in Bowels of Jesus Christ and I think if they are truly disinterested they will not desire to preach in the New Building or have the Articles altered. The Count sent word He did not use to preach without my leave. I answered I would consent if the other Trustees would, but thought it best not to preach till I came over. This is my opinion now.

[Charles Brockden to Thomas Noble, July 31, 1743.]

Dear Brother Noble,

Brother Evans communicating the contents of yours to him with Mr. Whitefield to the Trustees I was for a Moment at a loss what to determine, but turning to the words of the day viz. 28 instant I found it All are Yours and You are Christ's. I come to this Resolve not to be anxious about the matters concerning the Building or Brother Whitefield or any other thing, as indeed I formerly thought on the like occasions. Can we commit the salvation of our Souls to our Saviour? and will we not trust him with lesser matters or is Mr. Whitefield of so great consequence that our Saviour cannot carry on his work on Earth without him? Far be the thought from any of us. It's clear that our dear Lord useth him to rouze and awaken but to build up and establish he makes use of other Labourers. Whatever becomes of the Building of our Interests, Estates bodily Health or any other thing which we call ours, let us approve ourselves faithful to him whose we are and he will bring about such things as we poor Dust can't achieve by all our Powers. I admire Mr. W[hitefield]s letter of the 20. 7th should be so long in coming to your hands. I can't concurr with you in secreting it from the rest of the Trustees we should think we had cause to complain of them for such usage. Mr. W[hitefield] seems quite to mistake the nature of the Trust concerning the New Building whose use is declared to be Cath-olick not Calvinistick. He also exceeds the limits of his trust if he thinks to appoint schoolmasters against the minds of the other trustees or without them as though that were his particular Prerogative or Province. I had formerly thought of conveying to Posterity an Eulogium on Mr. W[hitefield] engraven on a Copperplate to be hid in the wall of that house. But I desisted lest it should offend the Lord and I wish in my heart the Splen-dour of these outward things may not too much affect the heart of the dear man.

I think then subscribing the Articles gives no one a right to preach in the New Building but the Persons being introduced by the Trustees and for my own part I never introduced any save Mr. Whitefield and I think none have been introduced according to the Nature of our constitution and that though a person were so introduced yet for a sufficient cause shewn the Trustees may forbid his Continuance. If the Trustees have any authority at all which I doubt they have not but the Proprietors and contributors only. Therefore were it practicable the only way would be to find out who they are and how much each person contributed and the use and design they intended and who shall be the Trustees to direct the uses which perhaps might be the way to open a Door for the Bishop of the Diocese to ap-point a Clerk. In short we are shut out of Doors at present and I see no way yet but was for leaving it till Mr. W[hitefield] should come. We might indeed forbid their proceeding in going on to lay out any more money on the Building or in the Burying there which I never liked. Or to forbid such preachers as we think not orthodox. But if we should and they in Possession should deny our Authority what shall we answer? If they object that we nominated ourselves to the Trust and were not of the nomination of the Proprietors. So far as a Trustee is Proprietor or hath contributed to the expense of the Building so far he hath an undoubted right and may recover by law unless such Trustee have tied up his own hands by subscribing the Articles which may perhaps determine him according to a law of this Province about Enabling Religious Societies to buy hold and enjoy Lands, Tenaments etc.

Thus my Dear Brother I have given you my full opinion about the New Building but not in that good Order and connection that a little more time might have administered. . . .

[*Charles Brockden to Thomas Noble, August 27, 1743.*]

There is lately arrived at Philadelphia from England one Mr. Benjamin Dutton who brings Recommendations from several persons on his wife's account as well as on his own and among others from a particular friend of mine. I have not heard him preach but from the little conversation I had with him I believe he has more the form than the Power of Godliness. Nevertheless at the instance of Mess. Hazard and Eastbourne and Brethren Benezet, Evans, Read, and myself we permitted him the use of the New Building under some Restrictions and amongst others his promise not to meddle with the Doctrine of Predestination. For my own part I complyed (as did I believe the other three) more for Peace sake than any other consideration. . . .

Suggestions for
Further Reading

No satisfactory general survey of the Great Awakening is available, although the century-old *The Great Awakening: A History of the Revival of Religion in the Time of Edwards and Whitefield* by Joseph Tracy is a classic (Boston: Tappan and Dennet, 1841). On the regional level the situation is somewhat better; see Edwin Scott Gaustad, *The Great Awakening in New England* (New York: Harper and Row, 1957; paperback: Quadrangle); Charles Hartshorn Maxson, *The Great Awakening in the Middle Colonies* (Chicago: University of Chicago Press, 1920); and Wesley M. Gewehr, *The Great Awakening in Virginia, 1740–1790* (Durham, N.C.: Duke University Press, 1930). A provocative analysis of the effects of the Awakening is Alan Heimert's *Religion and the American Mind: From the Great Awakening to the Revolution* (Cambridge: Harvard University Press, 1966). An attempt to place the Awakening in the context of American revivalism is found in Bernard A. Weisberger's *They Gathered at the River: The Story of the Great Revivalists and Their Impact upon Religion in America* (Boston: Little, Brown, 1958; paperback: Quadrangle). Also suggestive is H. Richard Niebuhr, *The Social Sources of Denominationalism* (New York: Henry Holt, 1929; paperback: Meridian World).

Transatlantic features of the Awakening are probably best approached through biographies of some of the leading figures, as in James Tanis, *Dutch Calvinistic Pietism in the Middle Colonies: A Study of the Life and Theology of Theodorus Jacobus Frelinghuysen* (Netherlands: Nijhoff, 1968); Stuart C. Henry, *George Whitefield: Wayfaring Witness* (Nashville, Tenn.: Abingdon, 1957);

and Luke Tyerman, *Life and Times of . . . John Wesley* (London: Hodder and Stoughton, 3 volumes, 1872–1875). Other biographies of important participants in the revival include Ola Winslow, *Jonathan Edwards, 1703–1758* (New York: Macmillan, 1940; paperback: Collier); William G. McLoughlin, Jr., *Isaac Backus and the American Pietistic Tradition* (Boston: Little, Brown, 1967); Archibald Alexander, *Biographical Sketches of the Founder, and Principal Alumni of the Log College* (Princeton, N.J.: J. T. Robinson, 1845); and my forthcoming *Henry Alline and the Beginnings of Evangelical Pietism in Canada* (Toronto: University of Toronto/ University of Laval Presses).

A number of specialized studies should also be consulted, especially Richard L. Bushman, *From Puritan to Yankee: Character and the Social Order in Connecticut, 1690–1765* (Cambridge: Harvard University Press, 1967); C. C. Goen, *Revivalism and Separatism in New England, 1740–1800: Strict Congregationalists and Separate Baptists in the Great Awakening* (New Haven: Yale University Press, 1962); Conrad Wright, *The Beginnings of Unitarianism in America* (Boston: Beacon Press, 1955); Leonard J. Trinterud, *The Forming of an American Tradition: A Re-examination of Colonial Presbyterianism* (Philadelphia: Westminster Press, 1949); and Perry Miller, *Jonathan Edwards* (New York: W. Sloane Assoc., 1967, paperback: Dell).

The periodical literature in scholarly journals on the revival is too immense to be listed here; a useful selection of articles for the student will appear in the forthcoming *The Great Awakening: Divine Mission for America* edited by Darrett B. Rutman (New York: John Wiley).

A collection of contemporary sermons is available in Alan Heimert and Perry Miller, ed., *The Great Awakening: Documents Illustrating the Crises and Its Consequences* (Indianapolis: Bobbs-Merrill, 1966). Other important primary sources include *Jonathan Edwards, Treatise on the Religious Affections*, John E. Smith, ed. (New Haven: Yale University Press, 1959), the classic analysis of the phenomenon of revivalism; Clarence Faust and Thomas H. Johnson, eds., *Jonathan Edwards: Representative Selections* (New York: Hill and Wang, 1935); and William G. McLoughlin, Jr., ed., *Isaac Backus on Church, State and Calvinism* (Cambridge: Harvard University Press, 1968).

A B C D E F G H I J   5 4 3 2 1 7 0 6 9